To my grandsons
Peter and John
may they, too, seek meaningful paths

Acknowledgments

I wish to extend my thanks to the Ramon Magsaysay Award Foundation for support and permission to rewrite and update these biographies which were published in their original form by the Foundation in the *Ramon Magsaysay Awards,* volumes *1979–1981, 1982–1984* and *1985–1987* (the latter to be published in 1990). The original material was written by Neal Donnelly, Anne Southard and Diane Umemoto, under the supervision of Marjorie Ravenholt, and edited by me.

I wish also to express my warm appreciation and especial thanks to Marjorie Ravenholt for her friendship and professional support during my years as an editor with the Foundation; to my husband, a Southeast Asian scholar, for his helpful criticism, and to my daughter, Marie Vance Hoy, who read my manuscript and found the work of these men exciting and meaningful. It is she who suggested that the techniques, developed by them to resolve problems in rural societies in Asia, can be applied equally to solving urban ills in our own nation.

My appreciation also to the Rockefeller Brothers Fund for a publishing grant.

MHE
Claremont, California
October 1989

Table of Contents

Foreword

In 1957 President Ramon Magsaysay of the Philippines died tragically in an air crash. The first common man to serve as head of state in the history of the Asian nation, Magsaysay lived as a man of the people. He invited his fellow citizens to appeal to him directly when they needed help. He shifted money from the military budget to education and social services. He instituted much-needed programs of land reform and rural development.

To perpetuate Magsaysay's high ideals of human service John D. Rockefeller, 3rd, and several Americans who knew Asia well proposed that an award be offered in his honor to men and women of any race and creed working anywhere in Asia in the service of human welfare. For most of the past 32 years the now-prestigious Ramon Magsaysay Award has been given annually.

Among the recipients are the noted humanitarian Mother Teresa, film directors Satyajit Ray and Akiro Kurosawa and the exiled Tibetan Buddhist leader, the Dalai Lama. This book tells the stories of ten men who are lesser known, perhaps, but no less notable for self-sacrificing and often ingenious work in the service of humanity.

All of them have labored in the field of rural development. We have a man in India planting forests, an Indonesian engineer developing water and fuel resources, an American missionary evolving a system of slope farming in the Philippines, a Bangladeshi professor of economics organizing a banking system for the poor and landless of his country.

Their work in rural development rarely is spectacular. More often it is quiet, unglamorous and little noticed. It tends to be vastly overshadowed in public attention by its counterpart mode of helping poor and distressed people—the massive relief activities that dispatch millions of dollars and millions of tons of food to regions stricken by drought, famine, flood and other disasters.

Yet the more rural development continues, the less we will need massive relief efforts. Reforestation can help prevent drought. Water development enhances agriculture and diminishes illness. Better village economies not only lessen poverty but also make a people more resilient when inevitable natural disaster—such as flooding in Bangladesh—strikes.

For just this reason, forward-looking relief and development agencies are trying to achieve more effective development projects to lessen the need for relief services. *Faith in Asia's Poor* goes far to encourage this important trend. By showing how development worked in ten varied cases, it assures good-hearted and generous-spirited people that development at the village level can transform lands and lives, and for this reason must become the greater part of our assistance to the developing world.

Robert A. Seiple
President
World Vision

Introduction:

Rural Development

The World Bank recognizes the strong association between rural development and national economic growth, finding that in developing countries where agricultural progress is slow, national economic progress remains sluggish. At the same time development organizations have noted that aid given at the national level frequently fails to "trickle down" to the people for whom it is intended.

Macro development projects may make a nation more self-sufficient in food or energy resources, but these benefits have frequently failed to improve the lives of large numbers of people at the lower levels of society. On the contrary large capital intensive, modernizing programs may further separate the poor, the untrained and the landless from the educated, economically more secure elements of society which are able to take advantage of modernizing concepts. A graphic example is the "green revolution" in wheat in Punjub which increased India's food supply and made participating land owners richer, but eliminated the already subsistence level jobs of large numbers of parttime laborers. Thus there is growing recognition that best hope for the future of agriculture is to refine traditional farming methods, rather than introduce complex and expensive new techniques and inputs.

Moreover, many of the nations of Asia are land poor due to

limited cultivatable acreage or degradation of the land by defor-estation and soil erosion. Faced with ever increasing popula-tions, the only way these states can feed and employ their people is to produce more food on the limited land and create more non-agricultural jobs in rural areas to absorb the population increase to deter immigration to already overcrowded cities.

Addressing these problems the Ramon Magsaysay Awardees attending the Magsaysay Assembly in Bangkok in 1987 agreed that development strategies must: recognize the relationship between population and the carrying capacity of land; take steps to preserve or regenerate the quality of the land; encourage aquaculture and household food gardens; acknowledge the role of women in rural life; provide credit to those in the lowest economic sector (women and the landless); make available pri-mary health care through a system of village health providers; and support a comprehensive family planning policy. If the last recommendation is ignored, the gains achieved in one generation will be lost in the next when land, productive enough to support one family, is divided among four or five heirs.

The men and women awardees participating in the Assembly were those who have pioneered such policies in Asia and have been honored for their contributions by the Ramon Magsaysay Award Foundation, some long before their philosophies and programs were embraced by governmental or non-govern-mental, national or international, development organizations.

The work of these practitioners offer valuable guidelines which can be summarized briefly:

• The conveyer of aid must determine from the ultimate recipients what they want and deem important. The transmitter must not impose his/her ideas of needs and values on the receiver.

• A donor cannot *give* a recipient aid. Recipients must con-tribute to a project by investing their own time, effort and funds (no matter how small), and must assume responsibility for the project's continuation.

• The technology and materials offered must be simple, easily available and replicable.

• The most disadvantaged societal groups—e.g. women and the landless—must be directly involved in any assistance program in order that they not be further isolated from the fruits of progress, and credit must be made available to even the poorest.

The ten men—eight Asians, two Westerners—portrayed in *Faith In Asia's Poor: Ten Paths to Rural Development* chose their own paths to help improve the condition of the people of the countries to which they dedicated their lives: the countries in which they were born in the case of seven, or in which they chose to work in the case of three. Each learned as he proceeded, and adapted his program to the needs of the people with whom and for whom he was working. With one exception all were highly trained professionals: five chose to give up well-paying, socially desirable positions. All have devoted their talents to those who, because of war, societal restrictions, or the vagaries of nature, have had little in life and few expectations.

Faith in Asia

Ramon Magsaysay Award Foundation

The plane carrying Philippine President Ramon Magsaysay crashed in the early morning hours of March 17, 1957, leaving the nation and the world bereft of a dynamic and dedicated leader.

A college drop-out and onetime bus mechanic, Magsaysay found his niche as a leader of men during World War II when he commanded a 10,000 man force of guerrillas fighting the Japanese army in the Philippines. At the end of the war he was appointed Military Governor of Zambales, his home province. The economy was in ruins, people were starving, banditry was rampant and the pro-communist Hukbalahup (Huk) movement was a potent force.

As a result of his success in handling the military problems in Zambales Magsaysay was appointed Philippine Secretary for Defense in 1950. He immediately launched a two-prong attack on the Huks, offering amnesty and help in rehabilitation to those who surrendered, but defeating in the field those who resisted. At the same time he saw that the army was properly equipped and morale boosted, but when possible used the military to build or rebuild the rural infrastructure.

Successful in restoring confidence in the government, Magsaysay was elected president in 1953 by almost 70 percent of the vote. One of his first acts was to establish the Presidential

Complaints and Action Committee. By the end of its first year the committee had received 59,144 appeals for help—personal, economic and political—and resolved 31,876 of them. As the Huk threat decreased, so did the military budget, with Magsaysay using the savings for education and social services. Moreover, unlike most of his predecessors and successors in the Philippines and in other newly emerging nations, Magsaysay did not use high office for self enrichment.

One week after Magsaysay's death John D. Rockefeller, 3rd, who had met Magsaysay the previous year and was deeply impressed with him and his vision, invited three Americans— Albert Ravenholt, American Universities Field Staff Associate in Manila; Wolf Ladejinsky, land reform expert in Taiwan and Japan; and Col. Edward Lansdale, close associate of Magsaysay—to discuss a memorial that the Rockefeller Brothers fund (RBF) of New York might establish in Magsaysay's memory.

The four men agreed upon an award program that would perpetuate Magsaysay's expressed ideals: that "government exists basically for the welfare of the masses"; "he who has less in life should have more in law"; and "a high and unwavering sense of morality should pervade all spheres of governmental activity." They also agreed that Belen H. Abreu, Legal Counsel of the Philippine Commission on Elections (the constitutionally established election watchdog), was the ideal choice for Executive Trustee. Her reputation for competence and integrity was unsurpassed.

The other board members—who were selected by a small group of friends of Magsaysay and expanded to include each acceptant—were Mrs. Paz Marquez Benitez, an educator, writer and publisher; Leopoldo B. Uichanco, Dean of the University of the Philippines College of Agriculture; Retiring Secretary of Justice Pedro Tuason; Jaime Ferrer, Undersecretary of Agriculture under Magsaysay who was later succeeded on the first board by Guillermo Santos, head of the Agricultural Tenancy Commission; and Francisco Ortigas, Jr., attorney, industrialist and wealthy land developer.

In the meantime (May 3, 1957) envoys from John Rockefeller transmitted a letter to the new Philippine president, Carlos P. Garcia, which stated:

"The trustees of the Rockefeller Brothers Fund would consider it a privilege to have a part in establishing a living memorial to the late President. They have authorized me to suggest the creation of the Ramon Magsaysay Award to be given annually to one or more persons in Asia whose demonstrated leadership is motivated by a concern for the welfare of people comparable to that which characterized the life of Ramon Magsaysay. To this end they are prepared to make available the sum of $500,000. . . .

"Those who receive the award should be persons to whom the award will mean encouragement for the way he or she has held fast to ideals and principles, even under adverse criticism. Each should be a person to whom the people of Asia could look for inspiration for their own lives. . . ."[1]

Garcia's reply, which constitutes a formal international agreement between the Government of the Philippines and the Rockefeller Brothers Fund, expressed his wholehearted endorsement. The Ramon Magsaysay Award Foundation (RMAF) thereby became a non-profit corporation under Philippine law. On June 17, 1959 the Philippine Congress made the RMAF a grant of land in Manila, which was equal in value to the RBF gift, on the condition the Foundation build a headquarters on this site within five years.

In the meantime the Board of Trustees made several decisions. It decided on four-year terms of office for regular members, renewable only after one had been out of office at least a year. To provide continuity and protection from pressure by other members the executive trustee was given a renewable term of nine years. Only the executive trustee was to be paid, and he (throughout read also she) would be the full-time administrator of the award program; the full Board, however, would be responsible for the actual selection of awardees and for management of RMAF funds.

The board recognized that in agreeing to an Asia wide, rather than Philippine, award it was venturing into unchartered seas. To investigate potential awardees elsewhere in Asia would require a tremendous amount of time, breadth of vision and

---

1. Published in the *Ramon Magsaysay Awards,* eight volumes, 1958–1984, p. 8. and Rockefeller Brothers Fund private papers.

analytical skill, especially on the part of the executive trustee. As the board members were aware, citizens of the ex-colonial states of Asia knew their former metropolitan powers far better than they knew one another. They were not familiar with other Asian cultures, accomplishments or value systems. Yet for that very reason, the board believed, an Asian award could play a positive role in developing regional understanding and would enhance the status of the Philippines in the area.

The board accepted the Philippine Foreign Office definition of Asia: the now 20 nations from Afghanistan to Japan and south to Indonesia. New Zealand and Australia were not included, nor the islands of the Western Pacific, although Papua New Guinea is tentatively under consideration. Although the Board has always been exclusively Filipino, it could choose to include other Asians by increasing its size.

The Code of Procedure, which was adopted by the Board in 1958, defines the five categories of awards and their criteria:

I. Government Service, for "outstanding service in the public interest in any branch of government, including executive, judicial, legislative or military." (No one in military service has been chosen to date.)

II. Public Service, for "outstanding service for the public good by a private citizen."

III. Community Leadership, for "leadership of a community, whether local, national or international, especially toward helping the man on the land and the ordinary citizen in urban areas to have fuller opportunities and a better life."

IV. Journalism, Literature and—after 1965—Creative Communication Arts, for "effective writing, publishing or photography, or use of radio, television or cinema [or theater] as a power for the public good."

V. International Understanding, for "advancement of friendship and mutually beneficial relations between peoples of different countries."

The award is "open to persons in Asia, regardless of race, creed, sex or nationality." In actuality the criteria are limited by the practical need for in-country investigations of candidates by the executive trustee. To date such investigations have not been possible in communist states—the People's Republic of

China, North Korea, Vietnam, Laos and Cambodia—and it is doubtful that these governments have permitted individuals to engage in independent social programs. Board members cannot receive an award nor can they make nominations.

According to the Code the awards are to be given for accomplishments during the preceeding five years. However, awards are often made for long-term programs that have come to fruition in the preceding five years, and in 1987 Father William Timm in Bangladesh was honored "for his 35 years of sustained commitment . . . to helping Bangladeshis. . . ."

An awardee is expected to attend the presentation ceremonies in Manila on August 31 (the birth date of Magsaysay) of the year he is chosen, and to present a public lecture in his field during the succeeding week. The purpose of these lectures is to make the expertise of the awardees available to their Philippine counterparts.

The Code of Procedure was modified in 1970, "prompted by considerations of protocol, logistics and security," to make heads of state and their consorts ineligible for an award. Not mentioned was an effort to avoid the political pressure that had occasionally been exerted, and the obvious fact that heads of state have already achieved public recognition.

An award in any category may be divided between two persons whose work is joint or considered to be of equal worth; in Community Service as many as ten persons may be cited, the assumption being that a board or team might qualify. Only one case of the latter has occurred. In 1963 the three leaders of the Bombay Milk Scheme, Dara N. Khurody, Tribhuvandas K. Patel and Verghese Kurien, were jointly recognized for "their creative coordination of government and private enterprise. . . ." An organization may receive the award only under the rubric of International Understanding.

The board has stayed within its self-drawn rules with one exception. In 1986 Radio Veritas was considered *a personality* and given the Community Leadership Award for its role in the support of "People's Power" in overthrowing Philippine President Ferdinand Marcos.

At the outset a decision was made to pattern, to the extent possible, the selection and presentation of the Magsaysay Award after that of the Nobel Prize. To help make this possible the RBF arranged for Abreu to attend the December 1957 Nobel presentations. The dignity of the ceremony, which concentrated entirely on the awardees regardless of the presence of the Swedish king and other distinguished guests, impressed Abreu, who replicated the format for the RMAF in spite of political pressures and Philippine customs.

In discussions with the executive director of the Nobel Foundation Abreu was advised against using national committees to select nominees; such committees, the director said, could be influenced and would usually select the least controversial candidates. Instead he urged confidential nominations from individuals in pertinent fields in each country.

The Magsaysay Executive Trustee, therefore, sends out some 300 "invitations to nominate" each September to persons whose advice the board has learned to trust and to persons who are recognized for their accomplishments in the five award categories, as well as to all previous awardees. (The latter have been particularly careful to suggest no one who would tarnish the award's prestige.)

The executive trustee evaluates all nominations received by the January 31 deadline each year, and by mid-February has decided which candidates appear most promising. She then undertakes the first of her two month-long tours of Asia, confering personally with nominators and others familiar with the work of the candidates and their programs. Traveling incognito—as a friend of a friend, journalist, social worker or researcher—she then visits each nominee and conducts an on site assessment of him and his work.

The first year's nominations show the breadth of the program. Selected in 1958 were:

Chiang Mon-lin, Chinese, for rural reconstruction in Taiwan (Government Service); Mary Rutnam, Canadian born-Singalese, for establishing women's village institutes in Sri Lanka (Public Service); Acharya Vinobha Bhave, Indian, for initiating the "land for the landless" movement (Community Leadership); Robert McCulloch Dick, Scottish founder and publisher of the *Philippine Free Press,* jointly with Mochtar Lubis, Indonesian, for battling for social justice (Journalism); and Operation Brotherhood of the Philippines for medical service in Vietnam (International Understanding).

The success of Abreu in establishing the RMAF on firm ground appears to be due to three factors. First her own incorruptibility. While the executive trustee's nine-year contract assures continuity and lessens pressure from other trustees, it means the program depends to an unusual degree on the commitment and integrity of a single individual. The very success of this arrangement under Abreu, could prove to be a structural weakness if a less dedicated individual is ever chosen.

Second, the decision that the executive trustee be a *voting* member of the board. Her input during selection discussions provided the board an invaluable insight into the interviewing and selection process, and did much to assure the wisest possible decisions.

Third, the continuing presence of Albert, and his wife, Marjorie, Ravenholt. In the beginning the Board requested the RBF to fund the Ravenholts as consultants. At the end of 20 years it petitioned to have their services continued, citing the need for an ongoing liaison between Manila and New York—to explain the actions of "one to the other" as only Americans familiar with the Philippines could.

Besides this quality of "interpreter," the Ravenholts also brought to the Foundation in its formative years their two decades of experience in Asia and a vast network of Asian contacts. They were able to put Abreu in touch with people in various countries and varying fields of work who were willing to serve as nominators or who were in a position to suggest others so qualified. (One may not nominate oneself.)

When the Ravenholts retired in 1984 the Board requested a further American presence. Mr. Neal Donnelly, formerly with the United States Information Service in East Asia, served 1985–1986, followed by Dr. James R. Rush, Yale University instructor and Indonesian specialist (1987–). Consultants are expected to live in the Philippines six months of the year, in two three-month periods. Besides serving as liaison between the board and the RBF, they have the responsibility today of writing and publishing the books of record.

Abreu retired from the position of executive trustee in 1984, and was succeeded by Dr. Perla Q. Makil, Director of the Institute of Philippine Culture of the Ateneo de Manila University. Makil died unexpectedly in 1988 and Abreu returned to serve as Acting Executive Trustee. In April 1989 the board chose Ms. Nona Javier, president of a Philippine mining corporation, as Executive Trustee Elect; she will become Executive Trustee in 1990 after a year of tutelage under Abreu. (Interestingly, the Board of Trustees, though primarily male, has consistently chosen a woman for the all-important executive position.)

The RMAF is located in the Magsaysay Center, an 18 story building fronting on Manila Bay. The ground floor and low wing of the L-shaped structure are occupied by the RMAF; income from the tower floors pays for building maintenance, staff salaries and program, and provides for the initial US$10,000 per individual award. A trust, established by the RBF in 1976 and increased in 1987, made it possible to increase the awards to US$20,000 and subsequently US$30,000.

For a number of years the idea of publishing the biographies of awardees was considered, but the project was not begun until 1975 when Marjorie Ravenholt volunteered to take on the daunting job: the Foundation was, by then, 18 years old, with 92 awardees. Ravenholt completed the first volume (1958–1962) of *The Ramon Magsaysay Awards* in 1977. Data for the biographies was gleaned from materials collected during the investigation of the nominees. Since 1978 the available data has also included a four to eight hour taped interview given by each awardee during the week of the Award Ceremonies. All biographies are submitted to awardees for approval before publication. Eight volumes (the last seven in three-year increments) have been published; the ninth (1985–1987) will be available in 1990.

These books of record have been distributed without cost to some 1,500 libraries and institutions of higher learning throughout Asia and to American universities which have programs in Asian Studies. Plans are underway to publish future biographies in individual—as well as book—form, to make them readily available for those with a particular field of interest (e.g. rural development, ethics in government). The individual biographies will probably be sold at cost.

In connection with an assembly held in Bangkok in 1987 to

celebrate the 30th anniversary of the RMAF, the Foundation published *My Work, My Teacher,* essays by 26 former awardees who were asked to comment on what they had learned in their varied work experiences. With one exception (Akhter Hameed Khan, 1963 awardee for rural development in Pakistan) all still had a positive outlook on life and faith in human goodness. And all who were engaged in improving the economic and social lot of their fellowman had found—sometimes by trial and error—that people must be involved in their own improvement or such efforts could not be sustained.

In recognition of its role in Asia, the RMAF has received funding to conduct regional seminars by such agencies as the UN Food and Agriculture Organization, the US Agency for International Development, the Philippine Population Council, and the US Regional Economic Development Office, Bangkok. The first seminar, held in December 1971, was entitled "Effective Partnership for Growth: Use and Abuse of AID in Achieving Asian Rural Development Goals"; nine awardees and six resource persons participated. The second, "Effects of Agricultural Innovations in Asia on Population Trends," was held the following year; the 3rd and 4th seminars (1984 and 1985) discussed election procedures and the problems of land degradation.

It may be interesting at this point to look briefly at the profile of awardees. Not surprisingly, considering the position of women in most Asian countries, only 26 awards have been given to women, i.e. 16.25 percent of the 160 awards made from 1958 through 1988. Twelve awards have gone to organizations (7.5 percent); the balance of 122 have gone to men (76.25 percent). Broken down by award categories: in Government Service 3 out of 31 awards have gone to women; in Public Service 10 out of 36; in Community Service 7 out of 36; in Journalism, Literature and the Communication Arts 3 out of 30; and in International Understanding 3 out of 27. (In International Understanding women were competing with organizations as well as with men.)

A further breakdown reveals that in the first eleven years, 1958 through 1968, 10 women received awards, 9 as individuals and 1 as a wife-partner; of the individuals four were non-Asian (Mother Teresa, Genevieve Caulfield, Welthy Honsinger Fisher and Mary Rutnam). Only one non-Asian woman (Elsie Elliott) has been a recipient since.

From 1969 through 1978 again 10 women received awards, all for work done by them as individuals. But in the past decade, marked by ever greater participation of women in substantive careers, only six women were so honored, three of them as participating spouses!

Among the men selected over the years, 16 have been non-Asian: 9 British, 5 Americans, 1 Dane and 1 Spaniard. Of the Americans, all were chosen in the last decade, and more surprising in this increasingly secular age, all are missionaries (four Catholic priests and a Baptist minister). Three American organizations have also been recipients: CARE, the Peace Corps in Asia and the Summer Institute of Linguistics.

The largest number of awards, male or female, have gone to Indians (23), and in descending order to Filipinos (17), Japanese (14) and Indonesians (13). Of the nations eligible, only Brunei and Afghanistan are unrepresented. On five separate occasions the board declined to grant awards because of lack of qualified candidates, and no awards were made in 1970 in acquiescence to the Philippine government's appeal to save foreign exchange.

"To celebrate the 30th Anniversary of the Ramon Magsaysay Award," an Assembly was held in Bangkok November 12–14, 1987, bringing awardees together for three days to discuss problems common to most Asian societies. The Assembly, sponsored by the RBF and organized under its direction by Marjorie Ravenholt, was attended by 90 of the 130 living awardees; most of those not present were absent because of advanced age or ill health. Also participating were past and present RMAF trustees (10); RBF officers (5) and trustees (17); and selected staff. Chairing the Assembly was David Rockefeller; Honorary Deputy Chairmen were former Philippine Undersecretary of Agriculture and Natural Resources Dioscoro L. Umali, representing the RMAF; and Dr. Prawase Wasi representing the awardees and Thailand, the host country.

Participants were assigned to one of four symposia on the basis of their expertise, and the questions for discussion were sent in advance with the request that participants come prepared to address them. The seminars were devoted to Rural Environment; Urban Environment; Culture, Education and Religion; and Peace and Security. Following two full days of frank and substantive interchange, summaries of the discussions and resultant proposals of each seminar were presented to the Assembly at large.

The symposium on Rural Environment recommended that: national economic development strategies recognize the relationship between population and the carrying capacity of land; steps be taken to preserve or regenerate the quality of land and encourage aquaculture, household food gardens, and family planning; and the role of women in rural society be recognized. Governments, the seminar stressed, should collaborate with non-governmental sectors at all levels and accept the validity of the experiences of non-governmental associations; "adopt a development ethos" that puts an emphasis on people as well as resources, with a concern for long-term benefits as well as short; excite youth as to rural possibilities, and reverse the "brain drain" to the cities.

The symposium on Urban Environment recognized that "the extreme problems of our cities originate in the countryside, hence they must be solved there," with regional towns offering income-generating opportunities and modern social services commensurate with those of urban centers. In the cities priority should be given to creating humane communities, serving all elements of society, including squatters and slum dwellers and should reject the separation of home, market and the workplace. Housing for the poor, education, and health care for children must be a public responsibility, but government policies should promote economic self-reliance and mitigate against permanent dependence on public subsidies. Planning and spending should be done locally, and society should combine the best of traditional cultures with the best of Western technology.

The symposium on Culture, Education and Religion, echoing Urban Environment, called for preserving and re-instilling among youth the best of traditional civilizations, accepting and adapting Western technology and economic planning, and reconciling the two. It called for respecting the cultural values of minorities; encouraging informational and cultural exchange across national boundaries; creating an environment for understanding the inevitability of change; placing a balanced emphasis on material and spiritual claims; recognizing that decisions should arise from the bottom layers of diverse national societies; and encouraging Asian sources of philanthropy.

The symposium for Peace and Security stressed the need for "Asia-wide fora at the inter-governmental and non-governmental levels, to discuss socioeconomic, political and security matters." It noted the importance of local institutions and recommended a healthy partnership between central and local governments, and between government and nongovernmental organizations, with authority residing at the lowest workable level. It pointed out that political instability often results from the pressures of growing populations on limited resources of land and water, and called for family planning, environmental protection, and special help for the poor, the very young, women, tribal peoples, and refugees. Asians, it noted, have primary responsibility for solving Asian political and socioeconomic problems, and the seminar suggested future meetings to "further develop collective approaches" to meet them. It also recommended active involvement in developing a peaceful international order.

The overlapping of recommendations expressed by the seminars is noteworthy:

• planning, decision making and spending should be at the lowest political level feasible;

• rural development is crucial to resolving problems, rural, urban and global;

• traditional values should be retained, but reconciled with Western technology;

• active participation by those affected is critical for sustaining programs; and

• concern for the environment and for vulnerable members of society should be fundamental to all aspects of reform.

Addressing problems with which they were intimately familiar, and toward whose solutions each—in his and her own way—had been working, the participants knew that change is never easy, but all faced the future, if not with confidence, with hope.

For its part the RBF announced the establishment of a US$2,000,000 trust to finance the Program for Asian Projects

(PAP) which will make grants to the RMAF and to RMAF awardees to pursue the Assembly's recommendations. Acting as an advisory body to PAP in the actual selection process is the Committee in Asia, consisting of three former awardees (who serve for three years), two RMAF trustees including the Executive Trustee, and a member of the RBF. The awardees serving on the organizing Committee, which held its first meeting in June 1988, are Dr. M. S. Swaminathan (India), chairman; Minister K. T. Li (Taiwan), and Mochtar Lubis (Indonesia).

According to PAP governing articles, 10–12 grants may be awarded yearly, preferably to fund programs rather than provide equipment. Proposals must be submitted by January 31 of each year to allow the executive trustee of the RMAF an opportunity, if necessary, to assess the requests during her annual February–June field trips. The grants are announced in December.

The first 12 grants went to four Thais, four Filipinos, three Indians and a Sri Lankan. Five pertain to recommendations of the seminar on Rural Development, i.e.: 1) building housing for disabled lepers (India); 2) developing neglected villages (Sri Lanka); 3) providing materials and training for tribal families in ecologically sustainable land practices (India); and 4) training a core of farmers in regenerative agriculture (Philippines). Benefactors in all cases must contribute land, labor and maintenance, and "practice the virtue of self-help." The fifth grant is to publish and offer counseling on the legal rights of the rural Thai.

Seven grants, addressing themselves to recommendations of the seminar on Culture, Education and Religion, propose to: 1) inculcate a sense of continuity and value for tradition among urban Indian children; 2) promote environmental consciousness among Thai pre-schoolers; 3) assist Lao refugee children in learning Lao so they can retain their culture; 4) publish books in Philippine tribal languages as an aid to literacy; 5) develop a pilot repertoire of dance and song common to ASEAN countries; 6) provide cassettes and tapes of fine music for Philippine schools; and 7) publish a book on historical architectural sites in northern Thailand.

The Administrator of PAP is Adlai Amor, recruited from the Press Foundation of Asia, Manila. He is also editor of the new *The Magsaysay Awardee*, a 12-page newsletter intended to promote a sense of fraternity among the awardees by enabling them to learn more about one another's work.

Although the Ramon Magsaysay awards, as distinguished from PAP grants, are given without stipulations as to expenditure of funds, most awardees invest the award monies in their own on-going programs. Interestingly, however, four awardees have used their awards in whole or in part to establish programs in the Philippines. Three of the four are Japanese, and their response may reflect the guilt seemingly felt by early Japanese awardees because of Japan's occupation of the Philippines during World War II (for many years the Japanese routinely apologized to Philippine Award Ceremonies' audiences).

Of the three Japanese, Fusaya Ichikawa (1974), feminist and parliamentarian, set up a small student exchange program; Yasuji Hanamori (1972), consumer advocate, asked the Foundation to use the interest from his award to encourage consumer education in the Philippines; and Hiroshi Kuroki (1974), governor of Miyazaki prefecture, established a Grove of Peace at the Filipino War Shrine on Mt. Samat on the Bataan Peninsula. The Thai government economist, Puey Ungphakorn (1965), established scholarships for Filipinos to study the problems of rural welfare.

The status of the RMAF and its awards has grown over the years. Evidence of this can be found in Thailand where the title "Magsaysay" is added to an awardee's name, and elsewhere throughout Asia where the announcement of a national awardee is prime time news.

Unlike the Nobel Prize on occasion, the Magsaysay Award has never been charged with being "politicized." The Board has honored conservatives, like Horace and Lawrence Kadoorie, millionaire philanthropists in Hong Kong; Father Hoa, ardent anti-communist fighter in Vietnam; and Henning Holck-Larsen Danish industrialist-benefactor in India. At the same time it has chosen avowed socialists such as Indian political leader Jayaprakash Narayan, and Bangladeshi rural health innovator Zafrullah Chowdhury; exponents of people's rights like Paul Jeong-Gu Jei and Father John Vincent Daly who fight for housing for urban squatters in Korea, Bishop Fortich who is in the forefront of the call for land reform in the Philippines, Elsie Elliott (Hu) who speaks for the poor on the Hong Kong Urban Council, and Gour Kishore Ghosh (Indian) who was imprisoned for his journalistic criticism of his government.

Other awardees have lived their lives quietly, away from social conflict, establishing village credit unions like Rosario and Silvino Encarnacion and Pablo Tapia in the Philippines; recording ancient temple paintings like Lokukamkanamge Manjusri in Sri Lanka and Fua Hariphitak in Thailand; or writing inspirational children's songs like Yoon Suk-joong in Korea.

Together they stand with those internationally acclaimed: humanitarians like Mother Teresa of India, who received the Magsaysay Award 17 years before she became a Nobel laureate; philosophers such as Soedjatmoko of Indonesia; statesmen of the caliber of Tunku Abdul Rahman of Malaysia and the Dalai Lama of Tibet; and film directors with an understanding of the human condition such as Akira Kurosawa of Japan and Satyajit Ray of India.

Each has justified the faith of the Ramon Magsaysay Award Foundation in the ability of Asia and Asians to find moral and innovative approaches to societal problems.

Evolution of an Environmentalist

Chandi Prasad Bhatt

In Indian mythology the Himalaya is considered the abode of God. Kalidas, the Sanskrit poet, wrote: "in the north is situated the mountain of all mountains, the Himalaya, the soul of God, which is like a balance of this earth." This balance has been disturbed by mankind. Forest denudation of the Himalayas has resulted in ecological disaster. The effects of deforestation, first seen in the mountain communities, are now manifesting themselves in the form of flood, drought, landslide and siltation of water sources in the Indian and Bangladeshi plains.

Chandi Prasad Bhatt became aware of the threat of indiscriminate tree felling after July 20, 1970 when a cloudburst over his home district of Chamoli suddenly raised the water level of the Alaknanda River more than 18 meters. Some 1,036 square kilometers were flooded as roads and bridges washed away, and Gauna Lake, formerly 100 meters deep, filled with debris. Canals, which irrigated over 400,000 hectares in the Indian state of Uttar Pradesh were blocked. Since then ever more houses, livestock and people have been lost to floods; and reservoirs behind the great hydroelectric schemes that are the prime energy hope of the subcontinent, are rapidly silting up. Such degradation of the soil and water sources inevitably leads to degradation of the lives of vast numbers or rural peoples.

Chandi Prasad was born in Gopeshwar, Chamoli District, in

the state of Uttar Pradesh, India, on June 23, 1934, the second child of Ganga Ram Bhatt and Maheshi Devi Thapliyal. Ganga, a Brahmin of very high rank, was a farmer and a priest at two of the most famous shrines in the area, Gopeshwar's own temple where the Lord Shiva is said to have meditated, and Rudranath, much higher up in the Himalaya. Ganga named his baby son Chandi Prasad—gift of the goddess Chandi—but he was not to enjoy this heavenly gift for long. Within the year he died, leaving his family with no money, only a few head of cattle and a half-hectare marginal farm.

Chandi's mother worked hard to care for her children and to see that her son got an education, a rare commodity in the mountains. In 1941 she entered the boy in Gopeshwar Basic School but he had to leave at the end of his second year because she could not afford the modest monthly tuition of one *anna* (three US cents). Instead she sent him for the next five years to the tuitionless temple school to be trained in Sanskrit and the conduct of religious ceremonies. From the small donations he received for his assistance in religious rites the boy was able to reenter Basic School in the seventh grade.

On completion of ninth grade Bhatt was sent away to study for the equivalent of a high school diploma. He caught malaria the following summer while helping his mother graze cattle in upland meadows; when he recovered it was too late to register for the next school year. He decided therefore to try to pass his school-end examinations without further formal study. In the meantime the village elders began to promote a marriage for him with the daughter of a well-to-do shopkeeper. Although both Bhatt and his mother were reluctant, village pressure forced the match and in 1955 Chandi married Deveshiwari Dimari and took her to live in his mother's house.

Passing his exam on the third try, Bhatt became one of the few villagers in his area to attain a high school diploma. This qualified him to become a schoolmaster, but the small salary it entailed was paid so irregularly that he soon left teaching for a job as a booking clerk for the local bus company.

Assigned to a station at the end of a road being built toward the famous Hindu hill temple at Badrinath, Bhatt had the duty of handling the pilgrimage crowds. Among the pilgrims Bhatt met many workers in the *sarvodaya* (welfare for all) movement, an amorphous organization inspired by Mahatma Ghandi's exhortation "to work for the uplift of Indian society, beginning in the lowly village." Bhatt drew inspiration from these dedicated men. Using his holidays and leave time he began to travel to villages where *sarvodaya* workers were organizing meetings and starting self-help projects. By 1959 he was so involved with the movement that he sought permission to join a *padyatra* (footmarch) through Kashmir and Jammu led by Vinoba Bhave, the great Indian leader responsible for originating the *bhoodan* (gift of land) movement and a guiding light in *sarvodaya*. During his 15 days on the march Bhatt had the opportunity to absorb Bhave's teachings.

Living in an area close to the border of Chinese-controlled Tibet, and committed to the philosophy of non-violence, Bhatt responded to Bhave's words that, whereas an army could defeat China's guns, India's best defense against China's ideology was the development of citizens with strong commitments to remake their own society, for "it is ultimately the strength of the village which will buttress our self-defense." Steeled by these beliefs Bhatt decided to make a complete break with the bus company and devote himself to the service of the village hill people.

The following year marked a period of change in the Uttarkhand (the collective term for the eight northernmost hill districts of Uttar Pradesh). The increased threat of war with China led the Indian government to undertake a massive roadbuilding effort for defense purposes, and to make a lesser effort in developing the area economically. The influx of government military and civilian personnel put great pressure upon the fragile ecology of the Himalayas. Moreover, the new road and government building projects were contracted out to men from the plains, and the contractors brought into the area massive numbers of skilled and semi-skilled laborers, further straining the ecological support system and bringing little economic benefit to the hill people who were hired only as menial laborers at minimal wages.

Finally, Gopeshwar itself became the seat of government of Chamoli, which had been newly upgraded to a district. Thus

Bhatt saw the village of his childhood grow from 250 inhabitants into a town which by the 1980s exceeded 10,000.

Unrecognized for the danger it is, deforestation of the Himalayas accelerated sharply. As the population of the hills increased, so did the demands on the forests near the villages, which were in turn fast becoming towns. Moreover the demand for timber *throughout* India increased dramatically, and the road building that gave the military access to the frontier opened previously inaccessible virgin timberlands to possible commercial exploitation.

The British in 1917 had established a pattern of village and state ownership and management of forest lands. Although some forests were left in private hands and the forests near villages were placed under village forest councils, the greatest portion of the timberland was placed under the management of state forestry departments, in this case the Forest Department of Uttar Pradesh. While village forests, which were barely able to support the original village populations, were being cut down to supply timber and fuel for the large number of newcomers, and to make way for new roads and building sites, the state government was continuing to give cutting rights in the state forests to commercial exploiters, most of whom were from the plains.

Although he was to become deeply involved with saving the forests in the following decades, Bhatt at first was concerned with helping the hill people benefit from the sweeping changes taking place. With two or three colleagues he therefore organized the Malla Nagpur Labor Cooperative. The cooperative, with 30 permanent and 70 temporary members, competed with commercial firms from the plains for public works contracts. Since the co-op members were unskilled laborers, the contracts were for heavy manual work, primarily road building. Bhatt himself, refusing a salary as an officer in the organization, worked as a laborer at laborers' pay.

Feeling the need for more training for his role in the cooperative, Bhatt went to Varenesa (Benares) where the central coordinating office of the *sarvodaya* movement was located. There he sought training in the Shanti Sena (peace school) which had been formed to train volunteers for the Peace Brigade. Established by Bhave, the brigade was trained in first aid and fire and rescue work. Volunteers were expected to work also for peace, even at the sacrifice of their lives, and were enjoined to set examples of community service and leadership by strength of character.

Women as well as men could enroll in the Peace Brigade, and the initial training Bhatt received was in a course being conducted for women. This was his introduction to the role women could play outside the home; this also became the cause of a breakdown in his own family.

Neither Bhatt's wife nor mother could understand the deep-seated concerns which had motivated him to give up a safe job with the bus company and, in a sense, leave his family to fend for itself. Thus when he returned to his village in the company of women members of the Peace Brigade, and assisted them in organizing a meeting to explain the movement's aim and activity, his womenfolk turned against him. His own handling of the intra-family controversy led to a three-year period of estrangement.

Physically, Bhatt had already moved away from his family. The members of the Malla Nagpur Cooperative lived communally, eating together regardless of caste, and sharing the money they earned by their work. Part of their time was spent in prayer and spinning—which Gandhi had recommended to all Indians so that they could provide their own clothing. Now in addition to his work as an officer and a laborer with the cooperative, Bhatt devoted half his time to the propagation of *sarvodaya* ideals. He traveled extensively through the district, organizing meetings and keeping in contact with movement workers throughout the Uttarkhand.

On the afternoon of July 21, 1961 Bhatt was forceably brought face-to-face with the destruction wrought, not just by man, but by nature. He was traveling in the mountains when the bus he was riding in came upon a landslide where an oncoming bus had been swept from the road and into a 95 meter gorge. Trained as a rescue worker Bhatt stripped off his outer clothing and scrambled down the dangerous slope. He found 24 of the passengers dead, but some survivors were pinned in the wreckage. With the help of another man who followed him down he lifted the bus from the injured and the two managed to carry eight persons up to the road before the police arrived to take over the rescue efforts.

No more than six days later, while on another *sarvodaya* trip, Bhatt and a Malla Nagpur co-worker were informed that rains had caused a severe landslide which covered an entire village. They rushed to the site, arriving before any other help, to find that of those in the village at the time of the slide, only a child had survived.

These two catastrophes increased Bhatt's awareness of the dangerous forces of nature at work in the fragile mountain environment, but the concept of environmental balance had not yet become a determinant in his life. He was still concerned with the economic problems of the mountain people. Because the cooperative was under pressure from outside contractors, and could in any case secure only low-paying, menial jobs, he began to think of establishing forest-based industries which would provide better paid, permanent employment for men—to keep them from leaving the hills for jobs in the plains as was the custom.

In 1964 in Gopeshwar Bhatt formed the Dasholi Gram Swarajya Sangh, later renamed the Dasholi Gram Swarajya Mandal (the Dasholi Society for Village Self-Rule, DGSM). It was organized to create small forest-product industries and to improve the welfare of the community. Most of the leaders came from the Malla Nagpur Cooperative.

In the beginning the DGSM sought contracts to cut trees and set up a carpentry shop to make agricultural and other wooden implements. Although the society won four small contracts, the commercial lumbermen, often with government connections, began to outbid it, knowing they could make up any profit-shortfall by illegal felling. The DGSM was thus forced to look elsewhere for permanent forest-related jobs. The next venture was marketing medicinal herbs, which the DGSM purchased from gatherers and sold directly to dealers, eliminating the middlemen traders who had pocketed most of the profits in the past.

At the same time the DGSM and seven other village cooperatives in the Uttarkhand established small factories to produce turpentine from *lisa,* the sap of the *chir* pine. The scheme soon fell afoul of the needs of the large turpentine factory located at Bareilly in the lowlands which was 50 percent state owned. Not only did the village factories have difficulty in obtaining an adequate allocation of *lisa,* they had to pay more for the raw material than the Bareilly factory which received its supply at a government subsidized price.

The heavy monsoon rains of July 1970 brought renewed warning that the destruction of the forests was exacting a price from the mountains and the mountain people. The rains led to the severe flooding of the Alaknanda River and its tributaries, the drainage system of the Uttarkhand. In Chamoli District the entire village of Belakuchi was washed away. Flood waters destroyed roads and bridges, caused serious damage to crops and cattle and deposited enormous loads of silt in lakes and canals. Fifty-five people lost their lives. Carrying 20 kilograms of relief supplies on their backs, four teams of DGSM workers moved to isolated villages in the devastated areas to provide food and help. At the end of the long relief operation the organization prepared a report that linked the damage caused by the floodwaters to the previous deforestation of the region. Floods occurring in the next monsoon season reinforced these findings.

Nevertheless the DGSM continued to concentrate its energies on supplying jobs for mountain people. On October 22, 1971 indignation at the "two-tier" system of pricing *lisa* led to a public protest. The DGSM joined other village organizations in the demonstration in Gopeshwar, and demands were made upon the government. Not receiving satisfaction, Bhatt and the DGSM assumed the responsibility for voicing the dissatisfaction of the forest people.

Traveling throughout the district for a year to solidify support for his mission, Bhatt visited Lucknow, the capital of Uttar Pradesh, and Delhi to try to gain the attention of the state and central governments to the villagers' demands. Meeting with no success in government offices, he turned to the media. Sunderlal Bahuguna, a *sarvodaya* colleague, introduced him to some newsmen in Lucknow who wrote articles highlighting the inequity of the pricing system for *lisa* and emphasizing the difficulties experienced by the DGSM when faced with government apathy.

In November after Bhatt returned, the chiefs of various villages met with DGSM and cooperative workers and decided on a major demonstration on December 15 unless the government agreed to a change in forest policy. The government failed to respond and on the 15th more than 1,000 villagers from near and far gathered at Gopeshwar. Women joined the men. The workers declared that for 12 years they had, through the society, attempted to *live* with dignity; now they had decided if necessary to *die* with dignity. But again they gave the state one month's notice.

When by January their grievances had not been redressed, the DGSM began to consider ways to dramatize their protest, still seeking to work within the Gandhian model of non-violence. The complaints now included a refusal by the forestry department to grant the DGSM carpentry shop its annual quota of ash trees for the production of agricultural implements. The government had instead given the rights to these trees to Simon Company, a large Allahabad sporting goods manufacturer.

Matters came to a head in April 1973 when agents of Simon Company came to Gopeshwar to arrange for cutting trees in Mandal Forest. The DGSM began a feverish search for means of stopping them. Some hotheads suggested cutting the trees themselves, or burning the forest; others suggested demonstrations in front of local officials. It was Bhatt who proposed a mode of protest which was non-violent, personal and vivid. Let the people go into the forest, he said, clasp their hands around the trunks of the trees, and defy the woodcutters to let the axes fall on their defenseless backs. His strategy was accepted and the Chipko Andolan (movement to embrace), known in the West as the "Hug the Trees Movement," was born.[1]

On April 2 a resolution was drafted informing the government of the people's intention to resort to Chipko action if their demands were not met. The government responded by inviting Bhatt to Lucknow to present the DGSM case to the Chief

---

1. According to Robert A. Hutchinson, "A Tree Hugger Stirs Villagers in India to Save Their Forests," *Smithsonian* (Vol. 18, no. 11, February 1988), Bahuguna, a journalist, played the major role in Chipko, but the extensive investigation by the RMAF convinced the Foundation that Bhatt rather than Bahuguna is the moving spirit of the "Hug the Trees Movement."

Conservator of Forests and the Revenue Minister, the latter since forest products were expected to produce a substantial revenue for the state. He was also invited to attend a two-day seminar on development in the Uttarkhand. Although no definitive action was taken, Bhatt's summarization of the hill people's complaints led to the appointment of a Subcommittee on Hill Development, on which he served as the only non-official member.

Upon his return to Gopeshwar, however, Bhatt discovered that the disputed ash trees had already been marked for felling. Therefore on April 24 members of the DGSM led a group of 100 demonstrators into the forest to confront the lumbermen and company agents. Cowed by the size of the gathering, the latter left the forest without cutting a tree, but did not give up hope that they would eventually be able to force acceptance of their rights to the timber.

The government now attempted a policy of conciliation. It offered to give the previously requested number of ash trees to the DGSM workshop, but Bhatt and the society demanded that massive commercial exploitation of the forest cease. The society organized another Chipko meeting in Gopeshwar on May 2 to which village chiefs, social workers and political leaders of all persuasions were invited. The demands were restated: 1) a complete review of forest policy to ensure the hill people's natural rights to their share of forest wealth, 2) priority to local cottage industries in the allocation of forest wealth and 3) a voice in forest management and administration by the local populations. But for the first time the DGSM recognized that the forest had to be protected, not only from exploitation by outsiders, but from poaching by local inhabitants as well.

Almost imperceptibly the Chipko movement had entered into a larger area of concern—it had begun to consider the mountain people as guardians of judicious forest use. Forest preservation and the well-being of the people were so closely meshed, it reasoned, that both could be assured only by making the people the forest's beneficiaries, and, simultaneously, active participants in its safeguarding.

Continued Chipko agitation brought further attempts at compromise. Government officials informed Bhatt that Simon Company's permit to cut trees at Mandal would be cancelled, but let slip that the company would be given trees in Phata Forest instead. Bhatt immediately alerted a *sarvodaya* worker in the Phata area who agreed to enlist villagers of the region in a Chipko action. Therefore when news was received in early June that trees were being marked for cutting in Phata Forest the villagers set a watch. After three days of fruitless waiting for an opportunity to enter the forest unobserved, the company agents left.

In late June the government made a further concession; it announced it had ended the two-tier pricing of *lisa,* but it failed to agree to Chipko's other requests. The *sarvodaya* organizations of the entire Uttarkhand thereupon threw their weight behind Chipko and instructed workers to spread word of the movement through their villages.

In December Simon Company agents and forest department officials returned to Phata Forest. Bhatt and fellow DGSM members hurried to the area to rally support against the projected fellings. A wily effort was made to sidetrack the Chipko action by circulating word of a film being shown that night at a village 12 kilometers distant, a movie being a rare treat for the people of this remote area. The villagers succumbed. When they returned the next day they discovered the cutters had entered the forest.

With drummers in the lead, 70 men ran into the woods to find that five ash trees had already been felled, but the woodcutters, hearing their approach, had fled. After consultation it was decided that a 24-hour watch, manned in turn by one adult from each family, would be set to prevent the fallen trees from being removed. A rally was held on December 25 and on the next day agents were turned back from an attempt to reenter the forest. Another demonstration of 400 persons, led by 5 women from Gopeshwar, was held three days later. The vigil was kept up until December 31, the date the company's cutting permit expired.

Although both the central government's minister of irrigation and Prime Minister Indira Gandhi, had publicly recognized in 1973 that deforestation was the cause of the increasingly devastating monsoonal floods, the forest department of the state, which was judged by its ability to bring in revenue, continued to auction felling rights, this time in Reni Forest.

In January Bhatt traveled to Dehra Dun where the auction of cutting rights took place, but his arguments against deforestation were brushed aside. Cutting rights to 2,451 trees in Reni were sold for Rs.471,000. Bhatt informed the contractor that he could expect a Chipko action and returned to Gopeshwar to plan the strategy.

In February a resolution was submitted requesting the government to block the cutting, and an appeal was circulated through the Reni-Joshimath area protesting the proposed fellings. In March Bhatt wrote a letter to the chief minister warning him of the danger of cutting trees in the sensitive region and requesting him to order a geological survey. Although the minister agreed that "tree-cutting should be stopped immediately," Bhatt had come to recognize the dichotomy between public statements by politicians and actions by government bureaucrats. Members of Chipko's Reni Action Committee, therefore, continued to trek from village to village, explaining the necessity of hugging the trees and preventing the depletion of the forest. A mass demonstration of villagers took place on March 15.

An interesting chain of events now occurred. While sojourning in Gopeshwar Bhatt was asked to receive a delegation of forest officials who professed an interest in the DGSM. Their visit coincided with the day the government announced it would pay compensation to those who had suffered damages during the defense buildup in connection with the Indo-Chinese Border War. Payments were to be made at the town of Chamoli. Along with others, men of the Reni area flocked to Chamoli, leaving the women and children behind. Taking advantage of the absence of Bhatt and the village men, other forest officials, the contractor and his laborers set out for Reni Forest.

The bus carrying the workmen had sealed windows so that the men could not be seen, but when they disembarked at Reni a small girl noticed them and reported their movements to some women. Gaura Devi, a 50 year-old housewife, rounded up 21 women and 7 girls to follow the men into the forest. They caught up with the laborers, who had stopped to cook a meal, and pleaded with them to leave but were rebuffed and threatened.

The women refused to be intimidated. Finally the workmen gave in and started back along the forest track, with the women following. At a narrow portion of the path the last women to cross a cement slab—which bridged the gap where a landslide had swept away a portion of the track—dislodged the slab, sending it crashing down into the river below. The way back into the forest was now cut. The women, nevertheless, huddled on the path throughout the night, guarding it until their menfolk returned late the next morning and relieved them.

Bhatt received word of what had happened and rushed to the area to organize a rally—the largest in the history of the valley— to bolster the villagers' will to resist. At the same time he assured the woodcutters: "Our quarrel is not with you, neither are we eager to fight your employer or the forest department. We just want to save our forest."

The contractor's representative and the forest officials left after four days. This signified the end of the sortie, but not of the battle. The government fought back. An official protest was written by a forestry official in which the Chipko activists were accused of obstructing the work of the government and causing a loss of revenues; the official defended the cutting of trees as being part of the scientific management of the forest and no danger to the environment.

A six-man state government committee, appointed to suggest changes in forest policy, released a report in which the Chipko movement was described as "utterly senseless." The forestry department requested that police be employed to ensure tree cutting, but the district magistrate advised against such a provocative move. Thereupon, in an effort at compromise, the forest officials agreed to meet some of the movement's demands if the felling of trees at Reni was allowed; the Chipko spokesman refused to yield.

On April 24 the chief minister invited Bhatt and others to discuss the impasse. Bhatt suggested that a committee of experts be appointed to investigate the Reni situation and the minister agreed to set up a panel of geologists, forest officials, experts from the irrigation department and representatives of the Chipko movement. When it was suggested that a non-government scientist should head the committee, the chief minister and Bhatt agreed that Dr. Virendra Kumar, a botanist from Delhi College who had been a recent visitor to the Chamoli District, should become chairman. Bhatt and Govind Singh Rawat, another member of the Reni Action Committee, were appointed to serve with the group.

The Reni Investigative Committee started work on May 9 and was to submit its findings on June 30. However it immediately split into rival factions, each armed with convincing arguments for its beliefs. To end the fruitless debate Kumar suggested that committee members go directly to the forest to survey the situation. Although all agreed only Kumar, Bhatt and Rawat actually made the trip.

As a result of the visit it became apparent to Kumar that a larger picture of the region should be obtained. He asked for a two-year extension to study the entire area and its ecology. A subcommittee—including Kumar; V. K. Sarkar, the Director of the Geology and Mining Department of the state; M. N. Mathur, a plant scientist of the Central Soil and Water Conservation Research Institute at Dehra Dun; Rawat and Bhatt—began work on the survey in October 1974.

In other districts Chipko resistance inspired similar movements, often led by *sarvodaya* workers. As a result the chief minister established another committee "to make a comprehensive study of forest abuse in the entire region." Its members included Kumar and Dr. M. S. Swaminathan, then Director General of the Indian Council for Agricultural Research.

The Reni Investigative Committee presented its report in October 1976, corroborating the warnings of Chipko activists. It recognized that the entire Alaknanda River catchment area—in which Reni lay—was in such ecological peril that all tree fellings should be stopped for a decade and regulations enforced against the overgrazing of cattle and the building of fires in the region. Furthermore it recommended that areas below the 10,000 foot elevation should be reforested and suitable varieties of grasses be planted in the section above the tree-line. The government accepted the report's recommendations in April 1977, banning all tree felling in a 1,200 square kilometer area for 10 years. Felling operations in another 13,000 hectares of land were also halted. The ban extended far beyond the Reni area and was for five years longer than originally demanded by Chipko!

Later in the year forest department representatives arranged to go into another region with Chipko workers to survey the forest before cutting. In consequence the department agreed to add 161 square kilometers to the protected area. In 1978 forestry officials went even further, asking Bhatt to check in advance a forest the department wanted to auction, with the result that another 64 square kilometers were placed under ban.

As early as January 1974 the DGSM, under Bhatt's leadership, had taken a positive approach to forest maintenance and had planted 150 oak trees, provided by the forest department, in the depleted village forest near the harijan (untouchable) settlement outside Gopeshwar. This initial venture was expanded with the planting of 100 trees in the same area during the July monsoon. In the winter of 1975 the DGSM planted 180 ash trees, and in the summer the society enlisted the help of the Malla Nagpur Labor Cooperative and the self-help society of another village to plant 9,000 saplings on barren slopes in the Gopeshwar region.

By the summer of 1976 the DGSM was able to mobilize 150 representatives of voluntary organizations from all over the Uttarkhand to attend a 45-day afforestation camp at Joshimath where over 8,000 forestry department saplings were planted on dangerously eroded slopes around the village. In addition the workers built a 1,600 meter protective wall to prevent further slippage of the land. The forest department, impressed by the work of the volunteers, paid the group's expenses. Upon leaving camp the workers were encouraged to start chapters of the DGSM-sponsored "Friends of the Trees" and begin tree planting drives in their own villages.

During this time other Chipko actions in the Uttarkhand continued, but with a new dimension—the active participation and assumption of initiative by women. The village women, through Chipko, had learned that they could assert some control over the circumstances of their lives. It was they on whom fell the burden of finding and carrying wood and branches from the forest for fuel and fodder, and as the forest had receded their task had become longer and harder. For example, a study published in 1982 revealed that the average woman in Pakhi, Chamoli District, made two trips into the forest every three days, walked 3.1 kilometers round trip, spent four hours in so doing, and carried a return load on her back of 24.5 kilograms. In another village the forest was so depleted that women spent 7.2 hours on these chores, making three trips in four days.

The Chipko actions were now often directed against local as well as plains contractors, and against their own kinsmen. In 1978 the women of Bhyudar sought Bhatt's help in preventing wood from being cut in nearby forests to furnish fuel for Badrinath temple, the destination of thousands of visitors during the pilgrimage season. Although Bhyudar's allocation of forest land had been reduced, the forest department was annually auctioning off 800–900 trees for felling and even more trees were being illegally cut by contractors in collusion with corrupt village officials. Although a protest had been made, the department had marked another 645 trees for cutting and, adding insult to injury, had awarded the contract to a labor cooperative in a village 22 miles distant. Therefore during a heavy January snowfall the women of Bhyudar went to the forest where the cutting was in progress, seized the workers' tools and carried them off to the temple.

A village meeting, held with the aid of DGSM members, took place a few days later at which the *women* persuaded the *men* to join in a resolution to protect the forest at any cost. The department eventually acceded to the joint demand and canceled the fellings. The following year women in a village near Joshimath stopped the cutting of trees by fellow tribesmen who had obtained a felling contract, and in 1980 they successfully defied the men of their own village—who had agreed with a government plan that they fell the village oak forest and turn the land into a model potato farm!

Under Bhatt's leadership the DGSM had begun to concentrate its afforestation activities in a specific portion of the area that had been ravaged by floods of the Alaknanda River. On the basis of a survey the society chose a 100 kilometer square area which included 27 villages. The river banks were reforested and trees were planted close to village fields so that the women would have easy access to sources of fuel and fodder. Retaining walls were built to protect the saplings and stabilize the slopes. Small streams were channeled and steep slopes were planted with fruit trees and grasses. The project was financed by the DGSM, with assistance from the central government's Food for Work Program whereby labor was compensated by allocations of grain. Most of the work, however, was voluntary.

In 1979 the DGSM had also begun the organization of a series of Environment Conservation Camps which were conducted at specific villages during June, July and January. Villagers, students, men and women, members of various voluntary organizations, scientists and interested forestry officials lived together in the camps for five days. They built walls, prepared holes that would be planted with trees after the monsoon began, and weeded and fertilized previously planted saplings. All participants were expected to follow the strict camp routine; all work was shared. Ample time, however, was allowed for lectures on environmental and agricultural subjects, and the last day of camp was reserved for a discussion of village problems with government officials, an exchange which often led to positive government action. Participants from outside the immediate area were encouraged to share the information they had gleaned and to start similar projects in their own villages. Since then some 80 eco-development camps have been conducted, with the participation of over 6,000 villagers.

Confirming Bhatt's belief that the most effective programs are those which are carried out at the grassroot level, the survival rate of trees planted by villagers as a result of these camps ranges from 68–88 percent; the survival rate of trees planted by government afforestation programs is from 15–56 percent. Government programs chronically suffer from lack of continuing care and from the planting of inappropriate species.

Dissatisfaction with the kinds of saplings provided by the forest department led the DGSM in 1980 to start its own seedling nursery, using broadleafed trees which are better for soil conservation and fertilization than conifers which the government had been planting for quick growth and commercial exploitation; a sister organization in Tangsa village started a nursery for fruit trees. A second nursery was begun in 1986 and more are in the planning stage.

Bhatt calls the participation of women in the reforestation movement "essential," and the DGSM recognized their importance by selecting six women for membership in 1982. Quick to realize the advantage of rebuilding forests close to their villages, women have eagerly spoken up, discussing where trees should be sited and what varieties should be selected. Consulted in choosing trees best suited to the growing conditions of the area, as well as those most useful for fuel, fodder and potential economic value, they have selected trees such as walnut, seapnut, orange, cypress, china pear, green oak, mulberry, cedar and willow. Women have, moreover, borne most of the burden of the actual planting, which takes place after the dispersal of the camps when the monsoon rains begin. Some 38 percent of the volunteers today are women.

Chipko Andolan has gained wide recognition within India, and the central government has proposed adopting environmental conservation camps for colleges and universities. Chipko has also attracted international attention. In 1981 Bhatt attended the United Nations-sponsored Nongovernmental Organizations Conference on New and Renewable Sources of Energy, held in Nairobi, Kenya, where he reminded the delegates that: "forest dwellers cannot be prohibited by law from satisfying their basic needs from the forests. . . . Unless we find a framework in which forests and people can live together, one or the other will be destroyed."

Bhatt has been appointed "permanent invitee" to the Board of the Uttar Pradesh Forest Corporation and the Advisory Committee on Development of the Himalayan Region Planning Commission, Government of India, and is on the Board of the Himalaya Seva Sangh, an organization headquartered in New Delhi which publishes articles and holds seminars to bring hill problems to the attention of the nation. He is regularly consulted by forest experts and government officials, and has authored articles on Chipko and the environmental movement in general. His other efforts include a sustained campaign against the big irrigation and hydroelectric projects in the sensitive region of the Himalayas.

Nevertheless Bhatt is not a leader who seeks the spotlight. He lives at the headquarters of the Dasholi Gram Swarajya

Mandal—although he presently holds no office in the organization—and receives a salary no larger than that of the other members. The US$20,000 he received with the Ramon Magsaysay Award for Community Leadership in 1982 ("for inspiration and guidance of Chipko Andolan, a unique, predominantly women's environmental movement, to safeguard wise use of the forest") was earmarked by him for DGSM expenditures. At meetings and in the camps Bhatt is often seated in the rear, listening rather than talking. Yet all recognize in this soft-spoken, clear-eyed mountain man a practical, hard-working, dedicated and far-sighted leader.

The Gandhian Way

Manibhai Bhimbhai Desai

"Rural man is a wise man. He has acquired wisdom over centuries of experience of living a difficult life. It is this wisdom that has enabled him to survive all oppression, exploitation and difficulties. His experience, moreover, has made him look at anything new with suspicion because everything new to him has so far been used against him. He is also very possessive in regard to his land and livestock, and is not prepared to part with either even if neither is remunerative; he cannot forget that these have been the only instruments which have enabled him to survive against all odds."[1]

Manibhai Bhimbhai Desai speaks from forty years of experience working for and with the Indian villager. But he knows from this experience that with faith in those who are working to create change the villager is willing to experiment if he is convinced his needs are being addressed.

Youngest of four sons of a well-to-do Brahmin family, Desai was born on April 27, 1920, in the village of Kosmada, Surat District, Gujarat, India. His father, Bhimbhai Fakhirbhai Desai, as owner of 27 hectares of ancestral lands, was the leader among the farmers of the area. From him Desai inherited his excellent

---

1. Manibhai Bhimbhai Desai in *the Ramon Magsaysay Awards, 1982–1984,* Ramon Magsaysay Award Foundation: Manila. p. 45.

managerial talents; from his mother, Ramibahen, his strong common sense.

At the time of his father's death in 1927 young Desai was in first grade at the elementary school in his native village, where he ranked first in his class (1927–1931). He also excelled in sports and was a leader in the Boy Scouts.

India, during his childhood and youth, was being shaken by Mahatma Gandhi's *hartals* (abstension from work) and *satyagrahas* ("insistence on truth," but in fact calls for civil disobedience). Desai vividly recalls an incident that occurred when he was ten and influenced his life. Patel, a young man of the village, joined Gandhi's famous march from Ahmadabad to Dandi, where the marchers raided the salt stocks as a protest against the government's tax on salt. Instructed to return to the village and ensure that a pinch of salt—which had become a symbol of the struggle for independence—was distributed to each household—Patel chose Desai to help him carry out his task. The latter was deeply moved when the villagers bowed low as they ate the salt, and at that tender age he felt the call of Gandhi in his own life—the call to service and self-reliance.

Desai's middle and high school years were spent away from home. He lived first with a relative who did not hesitate to assign him a wide variety of household and garden chores. Far from finding work degrading, Desai enjoyed most of the tasks, including tasks usually assigned to women such as fetching water from the village well and feeding, milking and taking the cow to the village pond. His mother, however, was shocked and the following year placed him in the hostel of the Anavil Ashram, the philosophic center of the Gandhian movement. There he came under the influence of the ashram's founder, Dayaljibhai Desai, a close friend of Gandhi, and Brahmanand Swami, a philosopher who visited the ashram and instructed the boys in mental and physical self discipline. The disciplines he imparted included early rising and celibacy, both practices Desai was to adopt.

In 1938 the young high school graduate enrolled in Sarvajanik College, Surat, an affiliate of Bombay University. Although he studied engineering as his family desired, he was emotionally caught up in Gandhi's "Quit India" movement. On August 9, 1942 all the leaders of the movement were arrested. In defiance—and without informing his family—Desai left college and joined the underground; he spent the next 19 months derailing freight trains and blowing up bridges in an effort to disrupt British communications. The clandestine and violent tactics engaged in by the underground, however, disturbed Gandhi, who sent the young men a brief message from prison:

"Why behave like cowards? Come out in the open and do whatever you want to do and/if necessary/die."

The group obeyed. Desai stopped blowing up bridges and instead openly addressed political rallies and demanded independence. He was promptly arrested. Confined in the main jail in Sabarmati with common criminals, rather than with political prisoners, he refused to have his spirit broken. He made friends with his fellow inmates, many of whom, he learned, had become bandits as a result of the injustices they had suffered at the hands of the wealthy. During this year in prison Desai also read radical political literature, including the works of Karl Marx and Mao Tse-tung. The views of Mao impressed him, but his ideas were modified by discussions with a fellow inmate, Ravishankar Maharaj. Maharaj pointed out that Mao was not disturbed by the fact that the people for whom he was fighting were often not willing participants in the fight; Gandhi, in contrast, insisted that the willing participation of the people was essential. The goal of both men was maximum employment of people in a non-mechanized society; Gandhi believed this goal could and should be achieved without violence, through love and good organization.

By the time he left prison (April 1944) Desai had decided to devote himself to the cause of rural development. However, since Gandhi had directed that no political prisoner should make a major decision while in the abnormal atmosphere of jail, Desai returned to the university to complete his final year. At the same time he began organizing students for social action.

Despite his extracurricular activities, Desai was a merit scholar and in April 1945 completed his B.Sc. with a First in Physics and Mathematics. His resolve to devote himself to rural development, however, had never weakened, and scant hours after finishing his last paper he was on the night train for Bombay to meet with Gandhi. As part of his decision he renounced any claim to ancestral lands, realizing, as he said, that people place greater confidence in you if you have nothing of your own—no distractions, no private interests—and that in India, if you have sacrificed, "you can penetrate the minds and hearts of the people very easily."

Gandhi accepted Desai as a disciple in principle, but insisted he must first return to his village and forget everything he had learned. "Bapuji," cried the new graduate, using the affectionate term for father, "are you against eduction?" Gandhi replied it was not mathematics and physics he had in mind, but the elitist attitude, taught at the university, which assigned to the exploiter the highest status in society, and to the man who toils the lowest.

Desai obediently returned home to Kosmada where he began organizing the village for social change, but four months later he received a letter from Gandhi calling him to Sevagram Ashram (Wardha District, Maharashtra State), the headquarters for the Mahatma's activities.

Shortly after his arrival at Sevagram a virulent outbreak of cholera hit the district. Gandhi ordered the ashram to control the epidemic, but its residents were understandably reluctant to venture into the infected area. Desai volunteered. Accompanied by two doctors and a group of 50 boys, he treated the ill with a saline solution to prevent dehydration, carried the dead to the funeral ground, and vaccinated those still well. The volunteers also taught the people to clean the village, boil their water, and cook their food thoroughly. These techniques stopped the epidemic.

Gandhi, recognizing he had in Desai one who could be entrusted with important tasks, nevertheless tested him further by assigning the young Brahmin university graduate the task of cleaning the ashram latrines and making compost from excrement and trash. After a month and a half, when Gandhi was sure of his disciple's willingness to carry out even these tasks of the untouchables, he invited Desai to join his personal staff.

On January 26, 1946, the day Jawaharlal Nehru declared the premature independence of India, Desai took a vow of celibacy so that he could devote himself entirely to the development of his country through service to the rural poor.

During the following year he became very close to Gandhi—a

man fifty years his senior—and Gandhi recognized that Desai was one of the very few persons willing to undertake the program of rural development which he, Gandhi, considered essential to the success of an independent India. Gandhi therefore chose Desai to establish the nature-cure ashram and development program in Uruli-Kanchan, Maharashtra, that he considered central to his plan. Although anxious to begin a rural development program in his native Gujarat, Desai agreed, and undertook the development of Goshala Ashram on 10 hectares of land acquired by the Gandhian movement through donations in cash and kind.

Gandhi gave Desai two general guidelines. First, the program should be labor intensive; a capital intensive program, he believed, would produce development but at the cost of increased disparities in income. Second, he must make use of all possible resources, even those that at first appear to be liabilities. Under- or un-utilized manpower is a resource, Gandhi reminded his young disciple, and year-round gainful employment for the farmer and his family should be his goal.

Desai last saw Gandhi in April 1947 when they met to discuss progress at Goshala Ashram. Desai, who still hoped to work in his home state of Gujarat, informed Gandhi that he had "taken an oath" to remain at Uruli-Kanchan for 12 years. Unimpressed, Gandhi responded: "I want your life-committed perspiration." Therefore on April 13, a day regarded by many Indians in the independence movement as a day of sacrifice, Desai bowed his head and vowed to "lay my ashes [die] in Uruli-Kanchan." Although his programs have spread far beyond the confines of that village, the Goshala Ashram has remained his headquarters.

Desai returned from his visit with Gandhi with Rs.100,000 to continue his work with the nature cure hospital he had begun, and the youth programs that were underway. One of his priorities was to organize the young people not yet spoiled by indolence or anti-social activities. A youth culture center which encouraged sports and dramatic performances was one effort; a secondary school was another. He began the latter in 1950, teaching 30 boys in his own cottage. Meanwhile he had started a cooperative bank to wean the villagers away from the usual usurious moneylender.

Desai also undertook to discover what the villagers considered their most pressing need. By sitting hidden near the village well and eavesdropping on the conversations of women as they did their laundry, he learned that the villagers were united in a desire to rebuild their temple. Accordingly he called a meeting and organized a committee to raise money for a new structure. When the committee was preparing to go to Bombay to solicit funds, Desai convinced them that by adding a school (his project) to the temple proposal they would be more likely to obtain donations. His advice proved sound.

By 1954 the new temple and a secondary school had been built. Rated nationally as one of the best schools in a rural area, Mahatma Gandhi Vidyalaya today has some 90 well-qualified teachers to instruct 3,000 students in its three categories of study—academic, agricultural and industrial. A hostel accommodates boys from distant villages. From the beginning the school was recognized by the central government and therefore has always enjoyed financial support; in 1980 it received a grant from the state in recognition of its performance and efficiency.

Gandhi always expected Desai to be resourceful. He had suggested, for example, that Desai take up cattle development to ensure a good supply of milk for the patients at the hospital. When Desai protested his forte was mathematics not veterinary science, Gandhi responded: learn the latter by studying a book on the subject—and by dismembering dead cows! The Brahmin Desai did both. He dissected over 400 carcasses and in the process became an authority on cattle physiology.

Although India had the largest cattle population in the world, it had one of the lowest milk yields; from an economic point of view the average Indian cow was a liability to its owner. But cattle, Desai came to believe, were a better choice of livestock for local farmers than pigs, sheep or goats. Pigs eat what humans eat, and in a land of scarcity compete with man for food. Goats and sheep, who like cattle can eat agricultural wastes which man finds inedible, graze closer to the ground than cattle, pulling up roots when hungry, and are therefore more damaging to pastureland. Good milch cows, he reasoned, could increase both the nutrition and the income of the local farmers. In 1948 he started a herd using the local Gir breed. The herd made such excellent progress that in 1953 the State of Gujarat donated eight top quality heifers, one bull calf and one adult bull, for the herd's further improvement. From 1957 through 1962 the Goshala Ashram's cows captured first and second prizes for highest milk yield in the country.

With the herd growing, Desai sought new pastureland, a scarce commodity in a region receiving only 8 to 10 inches of rain a year. He discovered Bhavarapur, an area three kilometers distant on the bank of the Mula Mutha river, where thin grass was growing under a sparse cover of acacia. The 25 families who owned the land charged him a mere Rs.280 for its use during the two to three month grazing season.

As Desai became better acquainted with these families, he suggested the trees be cut down and the land made more productive by plowing. The villagers were adamant: since the trees had been planted by their ancestors they must never be felled. The matter was not raised again for 10 years when, with subtle prodding, a young man from the area who worked the ashram's farm agreed to fell his trees. When the other farmers saw how much money he made from selling the wood for fuel, they too began removing acacias, thereby allowing the grass-lands to increase.

By 1965 the entire plot of about 36 hectares was cleared. Desai then suggested the families form a Joint Farming Society; they refused unless Desai himself joined. Since he owned none of the land he was not legally eligible, but the Chief Minister of Maharashtra pointed out that the law provided for 10 percent membership in such an association by landless laborers. Thus, as a landless laborer this former landowner became a member of the Joint Farming Society and was elected its chairman.

As chairman, Desai arranged for the area to be plowed by tractor and irrigated by water from the river using a jack well (holding tank). He could persuade the villagers to dig the well only by starting to dig it himself. Having lived in extreme poverty for generations these farmers had lost their motivation to work, or even better their lives; they had to be shown, personally, what could be done before they would do it.

When the land had been plowed and irrigated the soil was tested and found to be extremely alkaline, with a Ph factor of

9.4. A visiting team of American experts advised Desai to forget this plot and find another, but as he pointed out these farmers had no other. Instead he helped the society obtain a loan from the cooperative bank to buy wagonloads of gypsum, which was worked into the soil, approximately two tons per half-hectare. For the initial planting Desai chose *brinjal* (eggplant) which could grow in the still alkaline soil. After the salt content was brought down other remunerative crops were introduced. Today the land produces sugarcane, wheat, grapes and fruit worth more than Rs.300,000 annually.

During this period Desai continued his experiments on the ashram's own land—which had now increased to 33 hectares. Since agriculture per se was generally uneconomical because of the scant rainfall, Desai experimented with horticulture as a means of making the ashram self-sufficient and for cash crops for farmers in the adjacent villages. Research indicated that the dry climate and light soil offered prospects for grape cultivation. In 1960 he began planting local varieties, in particular Selection 7 and Bangalore Purple, and an imported variety which seemed well suited for raisins, Thompson's Seedless known in India as Madras Kismis.

Desai obtained 10,000 cuttings of Madras Kismis from a small group of families in Tamil Nadu who had themselves been given cuttings by Christian missionaries. One hectare in Uruli-Kanchan was planted to this variety. Desai spent 14 to 15 hours a day overseeing the proper manuring, cutting and training of the vines, trellising them to let sunlight through to the ground and thus prevent downy and powdery mildew from developing. Irrigated with the minimum amount of water for good fruiting, the plants yielded 38,765 kg. per hectare, more than the record California yield for the same variety. Local farmers speculated that the vines had exhausted themselves with the first crop, but the following year the yield was even higher. Today Madras Kismis is the most popular cash crop in the area, with average yields running about 22,500 kg. per hectare.

At the same time that he was experimenting with grapes, Desai was asked by local entrepreneurs if he would persuade some of the wealthy landowners in the region to invest in a sugar cooperative. He agreed on the condition that smallholders would also be allowed to join. With his help some 500 smallholders applied for a loan of Rs.5.3 million to invest in the Yeshwant Cooperative Sugar Factory, which proved a success from the beginning. It soon developed numerous branches and began engaging in other community socioeconomic projects, e.g. schools, hospitals and water resources.

It had become apparent to Desai by now that if the fruits of his 20-years of labor were to have a national impact, a sophisticated professional organization utilizing top-level managerial skills was required. Accordingly he founded the Bharatiya Agro-Industries Foundation (BAIF), which was registered as a public trust on August 22, 1967. Two days later it was formally inaugurated by the President of India in Pune, where central finance and administrative offices would be located and from which field programs would be coordinated. However, for the next two years BAIF existed only in concept.

In 1969 Tristram Beresford, chairman of Britain's Agricultural Society, visited Uruli-Kanchan and unknowingly became the catalyst to project BAIF onto the national and international scene. Although he had come for a brief look at the dairy herd, Beresford found time to visit the rehabilitated farmland at Bhavarapur and the rest of the ashram's projects. Deeply impressed with what he saw, he offered to help raise funds for the ashram. More importantly he procured, through the British Milk Marketing Board, a consignment of 7,000 doses of frozen semen from top quality Jersey and Holstein-Friesian bulls for the cattle project. With the acquisition of the frozen semen BAIF ceased being merely a concept and became a functioning organization.

Six veterinarians were hired and assigned to local centers that were established and supported by the Sugar Cooperative. Local cows belonging to individual farmers were inseminated in order to produce high quality crossbred animals. From cows which gave less than 200 liters of milk in a lactation, were bred cows that produced 2,500 liters: poor cows which had been a liability to farmers were converted into economic assets. The new crossbreeds are known as *kamdhenu,* "cows that bring what is desired." Insemination and crossbreeding with superior heifers was funded over the next few years by the Church of Scotland and the Danish International Development Agency (DANIDA).

The veterinarians at the local centers also trained farmers in the care of these improved animals. The concept of bringing modern technology to the door of the farmer, instead of having the farmer go to a regional center, is an essential component of Desai's development philosophy. His concern is always to simplify and humanize the developmental process.

As he began soliciting money from major industrialists to finance BAIF's dairy cattle programs, Desai realized that contributions would be limited unless BAIF qualified as a tax-deductible research institute. When he approached the Indian Council for Agricultural Research (ICAR) for certification he was informed that to qualify BAIF must handle at least 6,000 head of cattle. Frustrated, he was returning home to Uruli-Kanchan when he met with an accident and broke both of his legs. During his three-months in bed Desai devised a way to meet the ICAR requirements: he would request permission of the thousands of farmers in the region to use their cows for research purposes, promising the owners any benefits that might accrue from the project. A few months after his recovery, and armed with a list of 11,000 promised cows, Desai obtained recognition of BAIF as a tax-exempt research institute.

Two subsidiary research centers were established under the BAIF umbrella in 1971. The Research Institute for Cattle and Agricultural Development was started in Maharashtra on 40 hectares of land donated by the government; it now has 120 hectares. Supporting the development institute is the Research Institute for Animal Health. With a donation of equipment from DANIDA the latter began producing vaccine for foot and mouth disease in 1974.

Three years later the Indian Ministry of Agriculture approved a recommendation by the Planning Commission to entrust BAIF with the production of 100,000 crossbred cows in areas under the government's Drought Prone Area Program. National and state governments shared the operating expenditures of the centers—each of which was responsible for registering at least 2,000 conceptions of local cows during a five-year cross-breeding program. The infrastructure for chilling, collecting and marketing milk from the new breed of cows had already been established in most of the states. Although the annual cost of operating each center was Rs.60,000, the expense was covered by the guaranteed output in terms of pregnant cows. The income generated by the milk produced by the new cows was more than 10 times the expense incurred by farmers for the foundation's services.

Meanwhile Desai had begun to experiment with dry-soil trees, planting 10,000 shade trees on a 58 hectare plot given him by the government. Knowing that roots of a young plant draw only the water they need, he covered the area around each seedling with black plastic to prevent evaporation, and moistened the soil under it with one small glass of water every tenth day, later increasing the time span to every fourteen days. Six drums of water daily, taken from a nearby well, sufficed to irrigate all 10,000 plants. As the trees grew the dribble-circumference was extended; only the root tips continued to be watered. Ten years later the height of these trees averaged 10 meters.

Following his strategy of optimizing resources, Desai next looked for a plant that could be used for fodder that would not only grow with scant water in extremely poor soil, but could, as a legume, enrich that soil by drawing nitrogen from the air. In 1974 he received an ounce of seeds of the Hawaiian Giant (K-8) variety of *Leucaena leucocephala* from the University of Hawaii. This tree had all the desired characteristics—including rapid growth. (Desai had learned that a program to eradicate poverty must show quick results or those targeted by the program lose confidence in it.) *Subabul,* as it is known in India, has proven to be a quick growing and easily renewable source of fuel, building materials and animal fodder.

For its valuable nitrogen-fixing action in the soil to take place a certain rhizobia (bacteria) must be active in the nodules of the plant's roots. BAIF's laboratories have produced very effective rhizobia cultures for use in both acidic and alkaline soils which are supplied to farmers with the *Leucaena* seeds. In addition BAIF researchers have found that sulfa phosphate is a critical requirement of *subabul* and it too is supplied when seedlings are sold. The foundation now has a 162-hectare plantation of *Leucaena* at Uruli-Kanchan and a 81-hectare farm in northern Gujarat. The latter is irrigated with extremely brackish water—having 5,000 parts of salt per million (tolerable brackishness is usually considered 1,200 ppm)—yet the *Leucaena* is growing well.

Through experimentation BAIF has standardized *Leucaena* planting-cutting patterns according to intended plant usage. If fodder alone is desired seeds are planted close together in a row, with a less than a half-meter between rows; branches are cut every 40 days. Animals are not allowed to graze the plants because the mimosine (toxic amino acid) content of the leaf tips is high and animals which eat the leaves sicken and/or abort. This is not a problem when the whole branch is chopped up and, preferably, mixed with other plants.

If the *Leucaena* is to be used for building materials it is planted at least three meters from its neighbors and allowed to grow for approximately three years before cutting. Where trees will be used for fuel, two meters between rows is optimal, with a half-meter between plants; these trees are cut every three years. If these plots are prepared in rotation, one-third of the crop can be harvested annually. The wood can be used as sticks, made into an excellent charcoal, or converted into steam to run a turbine or boiler. An Indian farm family can thus satisfy its fuel needs with a small biomass plot.

In areas where *Leucaena* has been used for afforestation, and has been growing for a long period of time, the rocky, barren soil has been converted into humus. BAIF is promoting permanent agro-forestry arrangements of intercropping rows of *Leucaena*—planted about five meters apart and pruned to a suitable height—with a grain crop. It has distributed tons of the Hawaiian Giant seed to more than 6,000 villages under its centers, and over 25 tons to thousands of other villages through their state governments.

In 1980 BAIF started experimenting with sericulture as a complement to the established dairy program. Mulberry trees, to provide food for the silkworms, were interplanted with *Leucaena*. The two projects provide employment for the farmer's entire family. Cooperative units for processing the silkworm cocoons have been developed.

Also in 1980 Prime Minister Indira Gandhi combined all rural development programs into the Integrated Rural Development Program (IRDP) on a nationwide basis. This meant that BAIF was no longer confined to Drought Prone Areas. Its expansion was rapid. By 1988 it was operating in six states, with 500 centers and a massive extension network.

A recent BAIF program is with the backward tribal peoples of South Gujarat, where families have been given a one-hectare plot of wasteland on a usufruct basis. More than 1,000,000 forest trees and 35,000 fruit trees have been planted in this region and are well established. The innovative agro-forestry efforts have resulted in increased food, fodder, fuel and timber for the people of the tribal area, and equally importantly in year-round employment.

BAIF's decision to decentralize—establishing 10 separate organizations, each responsible for 50 centers—has required very strong coordination from foundation headquarters. This is possible because BAIF has been a pioneer among voluntary non-profit, non-governmental organizations in its emphasis on professional management and on financial control systems. The man chiefly responsible for this professionalism is Madhukar P. Marathe, chief finance manager and secretary of the BAIF trust who, having been associated with Desai since 1946, joined BAIF full time in the early 1970s when the scope of its operations widened.

Today BAIF operates on a three-tiered system. The operating agency is BAIF itself, which works at the grassroots level. At the second level is a sponsoring agency, usually one of India's main industrial houses such as the Mafatlal and Kirloskar groups. After a given project—e.g. *Leucaena* research—is approved by the government, BAIF approaches an industrial firm to underwrite the project on a tax-deductible basis. In general the money solicited is for a specific period of time and is designated for the establishment of infrastructure. At the end of the designated period the project is expected to be self-sufficient with regard to normal operating expenses.

The third level consists of a monitoring agency, consisting of experts in the field of a particular project. These outside volunteer consultants are asked to evaluate the progress and effectiveness of a program. Although most of the consultants are technical experts, BAIF has utilized the service of sociologists to define and measure socioeconomic growth in regions where it is working.

Despite the size and ever-increasing sophistication of BAIF, Desai never ceases to remind his highly educated staff that the focus of their work is not research, but the man who benefits from it.

> "We in BAIF," he wrote in the *BAIF Journal* several years ago, "have never looked down on the rural people as either pitiable or contemptible creatures. India's rural people represent perhaps the finest specimen of hardy manhood. They have withstood generations of exploitation and tyranny and yet retain love of the land, love of the animals and, above all, zest for life and the capacity to adapt to changing times. As such, we recognize the rural people as men richly worthy and deserving of being given an opportunity, as their right, to work for their own betterment. . . . The realization that we have the opportunity to work as partners, nay brothers, with the rural people, can certainly be our richest and most satisfying reward."[2]

Aside from heading the various organizations he has founded Desai has been director of the Maharashtra State Irrigation Development Corporation and the Gujarat State Rural Development Corporation; a member of the board of the All-India People's Action for Development; and on the governing board of Mahatma Phule Krishi Agricultural University, from which he received an honorary doctorate in 1977.

The President of India recognized his services in 1968 by honoring him with the Padma Shree Award. In 1982 he received the Ramon Magsaysay Public Service Award "for practical fulfillment of a vow made to Mahatma Gandhi 36 years ago to uplift, socially and economically, the poorest villagers." In 1983 Desai was awarded the prestigious Jamnalal Bajaj Award for pioneering research on the application of Science and Technology for rural development, and in 1986 the Bio-Energy Society of India gave him its first award for dedicated, dynamic and innovative work in the field of bio-energy. Also in 1986 BAIF,

---

2. *BAIF Journal*. Vol. 2, no. 2. January 26, 1982, p. 3.

under Desai's devoted leadership, received the Indira Priyadar-
shini Vrikshamitra Award for afforestation and wastelands development.

As one observer has noted, in his person Desai represents the
finest expression of Gandhian principles and scientific practical-
ity.

Missionary Farmer

Harold Ray Watson

"It takes thousands of years to build one inch of topsoil but only one strong rain to remove it from unprotected slopes," Reverend Harold Watson observes sadly. "It's a fragile thing."

Soil erosion is not a problem of uplands alone. The soil washed down with each rain silts up dams, clogs irrigation systems and causes flooding in the lowlands; much of it is lost forever to the seas. Moreover the forests which help retain the soil are vanishing at an alarming pace. In the Philippines the virgin forests are being cut at a rate of 10 percent per year, and hilly lands already under cultivation have lost nearly two-thirds of their top soil. At the same time the 18 million people dependent on upland farming are expected to increase to 25 million by the year 2000, and by another 12 million fifteen years later.

Farmers move onto newly logged hillsides, not only because lowland land is scarce, but because crop production in virgin soil is initially high. However these farmers, for lack of options and knowledge, resort to the slash-and-burn method of soil preparation and vertical furrowing, techniques which quickly lead to erosion. After five or ten years newly cut lands are depleted and farmers move on to repeat the cycle elsewhere.

Many are sounding the alarm to the problems of deforestation and soil loss, but fewer are trying to teach the farmers dependent upon these upland slopes how to protect the soil and its fertility and how to develop long-term agricultural self-sufficiency.

Harold Ray Watson was born April 17, 1934 on a farm 14 miles from Hattiesburg, Mississippi, half a world away from Bansalan, Davao del Sur, Mindanao, the Philippines, where he now lives and teaches. He was the second child and only son of Joseph C. Watson and Dorothy Mae Cagle, who farmed cotton, corn and watermelon on 32 hectares of sloping hillside land. His parents separated when he was a child but he, his mother and sister remained on the farm. The boy kept in touch with his father and both parents had a strong influence on him; both had deep religious beliefs and both were concerned that he receive the college education neither of them had enjoyed.

Watson attended local schools and it was his good fortune that one of them was Forest County Agricultural High. He credits his vocational teachers at this institution with directing him towards his future career. They emphasized "hand on education," taking entire classes to harvest crops, usually those of poor farmers who could not afford to hire extra hands. Through these experiences he learned two meaningful lessons: the practical application of classroom theory, and man's responsibility to his neighbor.

During the U.S. involvement in the war in Korea Watson enlisted in the Air Force and was assigned to Randolph Air Force Base in Texas in an office position. To occupy his extra time he volunteered to help with after-school activities for young people on the base. The satisfaction he found in youth work, and his growing personal Christian commitment, suggested to him a career in the ministry, but at first the idea was terrifying: he could not picture himself preaching. Nevertheless the idea grew, and his previously considered career options—farming and teaching agriculture—seemed less attractive. Eventually he gave himself wholly to the "call" and determined to study for the ministry when he was discharged.

Transferred to Okinawa at the close of the war, Watson traveled around the island. On one occasion he visited a Methodist Agricultural Mission. Although he spent only a short time talking to the resident missionary, he discovered that his love for farming and his call to the ministry could be combined.

Discharged from the Air Force in 1956 Watson married Elizabeth Joyce Daniel whom he had met when he was stationed in

Texas. The following year he entered Mississippi State University at Starkville. Since volunteer church work was central to the young couple's life, it was not surprising that a nearby Baptist church asked him to be its temporary pastor: in the Baptist Church an invitation to lead a congregation is tantamount to ordination. The work of preparing sermons, leading services and making pastoral calls was time consuming for a full-time university student, yet the young man welcomed this first step on the path toward his goal. He received his M.Sc. in Agriculture in 1960.

Watson had already inquired of the Southern Baptist Foreign Mission Board its requirements for a foreign mission appointment and learned that a candidate required a master's degree, one year of seminary training and at least two consecutive years of specialized field experience. With the first requirement behind him, Watson fulfilled the second by studying the following year at Southwestern Baptist Theological Seminary in Fort Worth, Texas. To meet the third he taught vocational agriculture from 1961 to 1964 at Forest High School in Eatonville, Mississippi. He then applied to the Mission Board for appointment and was accepted.

Several overseas positions were open and Watson chose Southern Baptist College in M'lang (Cotabato)—a small town in Mindanao, the second largest island in the Philippines.

The new missionary, his wife and three small sons, arrived in Manila in the summer of 1964 to begin a year of intensive Ilongo language training. The following year, with good grounding in the language, the family took up their duties at Southern Baptist College, which is provided professional staff and construction grants by the Mission Board, but is owned and administered by a Philippine board of trustees.

Since Watson's interest in agriculture was in the field rather than in the classroom, he was given the task of building a camp on 17.5 hectares in Kinuskusan (90 minutes from M'lang by car), which had recently been purchased as a center for youth conferences and church convocations. After constructing the dormitories and meeting halls he was appointed the camp's first director.

He was also asked to buy land and develop it into a farm to

help support the college. Choosing 50 hectares of uncultivated acreage near M'lang he planted it to rice and pasturage. At the same time he became active in the small churches in the area and in community work, building wells and instituting Christian Farmers Clubs where farmers could share agricultural information.

Thus his first four years in the Philippines passed. He had learned the local dialect, established the camp and farm, served as advisor to the college on many agricultural matters, and enjoyed his work. His children had adjusted to rural life in Mindanao and his wife shared his vocation fully and enthusiastically.

Nevertheless he was strangely dissatisfied, asking himself, "Is this what I really want to do with the rest of my life?" As he and his family were happy, the question seemed odd until he reminded himself that he had become an agricultural missionary to help farmers directly: to show them how to raise more and better crops, produce bigger and healthier livestock, revitalize soil and increase income. To be effective, he argued, he should not be replicating the work of others; his contributions should be original and direct.

In consequence he gradually evolved a plan for a demonstration farm for small or subsistence farmers, drawing on scientific information, but relying on local materials, expertise and farm experience. No agricultural technology, he had come to believe, was completely transferable. Every method must fit the environment and be in accord with local needs and customs.

In 1968, therefore, Watson approached the church board for money to buy a piece of farmland and learned to his pleasant surprise that funds were available. A U.S. businessman had recently donated US$1,000 for such work. Coincidentally a plot of 10 hectares adjacent to the camp was for sale. On inspection Watson found it an impoverished and denuded hillside, abandoned by slash-and-burn farmers, land which seemed far from ideal for demonstrating agricultural technology. Upon reflection, however, he realized that if such abused soil could be made fertile again it would be the best possible validation of his ideas. He accepted the challenge.

His first task was to build two small houses, one for his co-worker Rodrigo Golez and one for his family. Simple wooden structures built by a local contractor, the houses lacked the amenities of town, but well water, bottled gas and a small generator made living reasonably comfortable. Watson named the site the "Mindanao Baptist Rural Life Center" (BRLC). Here he proposed to introduce techniques that were readily adaptable to local conditions, avoiding schemes which required heavy investment, sophisticated equipment, or expensive fertilizers, none of which are available to the marginal farmer. The now famous FAITH Garden was the result.

FAITH stands for "Food Always in the Home," and is a blueprint for ensuring that, with a 100 square meter plot and a minimum of expense and labor, fruits and vegetables—providing proteins, vitamins and minerals for a family of six—will be available every day of the year.

The FAITH plan calls for one-third of the garden to be planted in lima beans, swamp cabbage, *camote* (variety of sweet potato) or similar vegetables which need planting only once a year. Another third should be in eggplant, winged beans, Malabar or Ceylon spinach and squash. These require replanting every six months. The remaining third is to be planted with seasonal vegetables such as okra, tomatoes and beans which must be planted more frequently. Finally, the boundaries of the garden should be planted with small trees such as the "horseradish tree," the papaya or the small green citrus called the *calamansi*.

Chemical fertilizers are discouraged. The soil is enriched through a series of compost baskets sunk one meter apart throughout the garden. Any basket or perforated container about one foot in diameter, one foot tall, and strong enough to reinforce the walls of the dirt cavity, is suitable. The baskets can be filled with whatever organic materials—home garbage, farm and garden waste, weeds or manure—are available.

Seeds or seedlings are planted two or three inches apart around the basket. Watering is simplified because water is poured only into the baskets. The organic matter in the baskets absorbs the water and releases it slowly, thus plant roots can find moisture around the basket even if the rest of the earth is parched. The basket serves a further function. It contains or restrains the decomposing material, thereby preventing chickens, animals and the wind from scattering the waste. After the crops are harvested the basket is emptied and its contents worked into the surrounding soil which thereby becomes looser, richer and more productive. The basket is then refilled with new composting material and the cycle repeated.

The FAITH demonstration garden at the Baptist Rural Life Center has been in operation since 1972 and is used in training 1,000 persons yearly in these simple techniques. Thousands more have learned this method through other BRLC extension projects.

In order to supply the farmers with protein for their diet and a marketable product, Watson next sought to introduce an easy-to-raise and inexpensive meat source. In this he was initially less successful, making several false starts.

He first offered the farmers varieties of New Zealand and California rabbits, animals both easy and inexpensive to raise, whose white meat tastes like chicken. A female, when fed a balanced diet including concentrates, produces eight offspring every two months. Watson sold his breeding rabbits for a nominal 10 pesos (US$1.40), which included the accompanying training session and instruction sheet.

Word of this bargain quickly spread and soon everyone was buying and raising rabbits. Watson warned the farmers of overproduction and of the necessity of developing outside markets but no one listened, or if one did he lacked the entrepreneurial talent or inclination to seek markets elsewhere. Consequently rabbits were soon in surplus and breeding enthusiasm waned, although some farmers still raise the animals on a more realistic scale.

BRLC next tried promoting White Leghorns and other high-bred chickens as a protein and income source for marginal farmers, but the expense and unreliability of a supply of quality feed made raising them a risky venture. Without consistent good feed highbreds stop laying; on the other hand, as with the rabbits, overproduction causes prices to drop. Large commercial breeders can absorb quantity and price fluctuations but the small farmer cannot.

Watson's experience with hogs was equally unsuccessful. Some of the world's largest hog producers are in Davao City, a few hours drive from BRLC. The commercial piggeries, quite naturally, discouraged competition and charged a prohibitive price for a quality piglet. Ignoring the cost Watson bought a few Duroc Jerseys which are hearty and withstand heat well, and experimented in breeding them with Landrace, Yorkshire and Hampshire hogs. Again, the drawback for the individual was the profit margin. Moreover, hogs are highly susceptible to diseases such as rinderpest, cholera and swine influenza, and a small farmer can lose everything if his hogs become infected. BRLC still distributes about 100 piglets per year, but Watson realized that hog raising was also not the answer to the small farmers' financial predicament.

Watson finally turned his attention to goats, which had the attraction of supplying milk as well as red meat. He contacted Richard Fagan of the Philippine Rural Life Center, Manila, who arranged through the Heifer Project of Little Rock, Arkansas, to bring three Nubian and three Saanan goats (two does and a buck of each) from the U.S. The only condition the Heifer Project imposed was that the goats must be bred and two given away for each one kept—a condition precisely matching the philosophy of BRLC.

After some experimentation Watson decided that the Nubians adapted to local conditions better than the Saanans and bought 10 of them. These form the nucleus of the center's present herd of 400.

The goats are raised on small covered platforms to prevent foot rot and parasites, and to protect crops and orchards from their indiscriminate appetites—goats will eat anything. The quarters are cramped, but Watson has determined that seven square meters is sufficient for each animal. The leaves of *Leucaena leucocephala* (called *ipil ipil* in the Philippines), rice bran and copra meal comprise their diet.

Nubian goats are economical; they are heavier than the native breed, and their milk is richer and thicker than that of cows. An average doe gives 2.3 liters of milk per day, with a lactation period of 225 days per year. BRLC distributes about 100 goats annually, but farmers must first take a course in goat care to prove they know how—and are willing—to raise them properly.

Ducks have also proven to be both popular and economical.

Through the Heifer Project Watson brought 25 purebred Khaki Campbell ducks from the U.S. His staff constructed an ingenious cost-free brooder from a five-gallon can; using rice hulls for fuel, it burns for 12 hours without replenishment. The ducks' diet consists of azolla—a minute water fern, and Golden Snails with which Watson stocked his stream. He estimates the ducks get half their protein from the latter.

BRLC maintains a flock of 200 ducks and distributes some 3,000 ducklings yearly. It recommends these or local ducks to the tribal mountain peoples. The return on the investment is handsome and almost immediate, since a duck can sit on 8 to 25 eggs and ducklings are ready for the table in only 10 weeks.

BRLC also encourages raising fish in ponds and has adopted the integrated animal-fish method of feeding. Hogs or ducks are housed in small covered pens above the fish ponds. Their waste and scattered feed drop into the pond, fertilizing the algae and plankton which in turn are eaten by the fish. The latter are an excellent source of protein for the small farmer.

As BRLC's reputation grew, more hillside farmers sought advice from Watson and his staff—which had increased to 6 professionals and 15 laborers by the late 1970s. The senior management staff by then consisted of Watson; Warlito Laquihon, former Dean of Agriculture at Southern Baptist College, who joined the project as Assistant Director in 1976 ("his coming was the key," Watson says; "after that we really expanded"); and Farm Manager Rodrigo Calixtro. The three work as a team, discussing projects and agreeing upon policy.

The team was long aware that the major problems of the area were leached soil and soil erosion, both of which were responsible for low crop productivity. The rural poor, typical slash-and burn farmers, were forced to cultivate upland areas to survive, and their excessive numbers had now made it impossible to allow the land to stand idle the usual 15 to 20 years between periods of cultivation. Instead it was being replanted after 3 or 4 years. As a result the forest cover had no time to grow back and leaching and erosion accelerated. Moreover, the traditional methods of plowing—vertically or irregularly instead of laterally across the slope of the hill—greatly increased soil loss.

Watson, Laquihon and Calixtro analyzed the problems they faced, enumerating the criteria for any eventual solution. They required a scheme which: 1) controlled soil erosion, 2) restored fertility, 3) relied on local resources, 4) required no loan money, 5) emphasized food over cash crops yet provided a farmer with an income for necessities and a cushion for the future, 6) demanded a minimum of labor, and 7) was easily understood and culturally acceptable.

After much discussion and experimentation they evolved a blueprint for a technology which met all the criteria. They called their new system Sloping Agricultural Land Technology (SALT).

A distinctive feature of SALT, an expansion of terraced farming, is the use of *Leucaena* to control erosion and retain the soil. *Leucaena* grows quickly and widely in the Philippines and BLRC had earlier imported the improved Hawaiian Giant from Hawaii.

Watson had always believed in contour farming and in 1971 he had laid out terraced, contoured rice fields at the demonstration farm. The problem, he found, was to determine the slope and drainage flow from one terrace to the next, and to prevent terraces from washing out. Recourse to academic solutions was fruitless. No technology applicable to slope land farming in Mindanao was available. The team therefore devised a method of determining contour lines by means of a simple "A"-shaped frame, with a string and rock suspended from the top of the "A."

They then planted double hedges of *Leucaena* in rows about six meters apart, leaving a space in-between for planting crops. The *Leucaena* was kept as a low shrub and trimmed when it reached a meter in height, roughly once a month. The cut leaves were then used as fertilizer for the crops planted between the rows, or for animal feed. As with the FAITH Garden the farmer was urged to alternate semi-permanent with seasonal plantings, rotating the latter between legumes and non-legumes. A good planting mix would be ginger, beans, rice, pineapple and corn—with bamboo, or trees such as rambutan, durian, banana and citrus, planted at the top and the bottom of the plot.

The demonstration lot, developed in 1980, was sited on one hectare of impoverished, hilly land with a 15 degree slope. To assure themselves that their technique was simple enough for any farmer to replicate, the team hired a tribesman with a sixth grade education to farm it. Using only hand tools, and working alone five and a half days a week with time off for numerous religious and traditional holidays, the tribesman successfully contoured the hill, planted the *Leucaena,* readied the soil and planted peanuts, mungo beans, pineapple, corn, bananas and coffee.

The demonstration met all the criteria Watson and his colleagues had set forth. It proved that hillside land can be farmed successfully and that a hectare thus farmed can provide a family of seven with a steady source of food and income throughout the year. A further advantage, Watson explains, is that because harvests are small—and spread throughout the year—the farmer does not need to hire extra help or sell through a middleman; he can harvest and market his produce himself.

A recent study estimates that a farmer using SALT can realize a return of 50 percent on his investment the first year, 104 percent the second, 131 the third, 207 the fourth and 415 percent by the fifth year. Cotabato SALT farmers report a P1,125 average monthly income from the sale of surplus crops as opposed to the non-SALT farmer average of P250.

Early in 1983 SALT's success came to the attention of the Agricultural Educational Outreach Project (AEOP) of the Philippine Ministry of Education. AEOP adopted SALT as a major technology for upland development and introduced it in agricultural colleges strategically located throughout the islands. These institutions established demonstration farms on their campuses and in nearby villages; ten other academic institutions followed suit. AEOP estimates that the Philippines has about 500,000 hectares of hillside wasteland which can be revitalized by SALT and made to support some 2,000,000 people.

Church groups and other organizations have brought technicians from overseas to study the Sloping Agricultural Land Technology and introduce it in their own countries. USAID has sponsored Indonesian groups, and the Baptist Church has brought tribal farmers from Thailand. Individual observers from Australia, Bangladesh, India, Japan, Nepal, New Zealand, Taiwan and the United States have also visited BRLC to study

SALT. As early as 1984 dozens of classes of three-to-five days' duration were being given to some 900 students.

BRLC also offers the farmers of Cotabato and neighboring provinces inexpensive and practical training in techniques other than SALT. For a few pesos a day a farmer can study crop growing, animal care, rural sanitation or any one of 37 other subjects. Accommodations, provided at the adjacent Baptist camp, are spartan but inexpensive. Those attending courses, most of which last only a few days, are asked to provide their own food.

Besides instituting classes at BRLC, Watson began a four-month, church-oriented, training program for farm youth called BOOST—Baptist Outside Of School Training. The four training centers on Mindanao offer agricultural technology, farm and home development, health, community organization, self-aware-ness and Bible study, along with practical farm work. Learning is by doing, teaching is by example, and teachers and students live in close proximity. Watson's motto is: "What I hear I forget. What I see I remember. What I do I know!"

Students for this program must be recommended by their churches. Transportation and food are subsidized but partici-pants are expected to pay a P10 registration fee and P15 towards transportation. They are requested to bring enough rice for one month; their meat and vegetables come from the animals and gardens they tend, and everyone does his own cooking. Since the program is considered work-study BOOST pays each student P25 per week; in return graduates are expected to share their knowledge when they return home. Approximately 360 young people are trained annually.

When Watson first began promoting raising rabbits, he pre-pared one-page instruction sheets on their care. The popularity of the sheets encouraged BRLC to compile booklets for each major project. At first the Foreign Mission Board paid for the paper and printing so the booklets were free, but because they were free people often took multiple copies and wasted them. BRLC now charges enough to cover costs. The booklets, aver-aging two pages, are printed on newsprint. There is no need to use expensive material, Watson believes, because a farmer will not keep the instructions once he has mastered the technique.

Watson and Laquihon write the instruction sheets in a direct, easy-to-follow style, in two local languages and English. To provide the widest possible dissemination of the information, a notice is inserted advising that "anyone is free to translate, reprint, condense and reproduce" the material, provided acknowledgement of the source is given; the SALT instruction booklet, for example, has been translated into Indonesian. About 20,000 of these "how-to" manuals are sold yearly. The subjects covered are: *Leucaena leucocephala,* legumes, tomatoes, corn, soybeans, pineapple, cherries, coffee, cacao, sorghum, ducks, goats, pigs, cows, pigeons, *tilapia* (a fish) and rabbits. Bookets also instruct the farmer on how to plan a FAITH Garden, make a basket compost, tan rabbit hide, build a bio-gas generator and control common poultry diseases.

To support agricultural outreach, BRLC produces a "Back to the Farm" 15 minute weekly radio program in three languages: English, Cebuano and Ilongo. Like other BLRC efforts it offers the farmer simple, practical agricultural information. It is carried by five radio stations in Mindanao, which together are capable of reaching at least half of the more than 10 million people on the island. Each program includes a three-minute religious or inspirational message.

BRLC has been recognized for its development of SALT by the Crop Science Society, the Ministry of Human Settlement, and the Farm System Development Corporation of the Philippines. Watson himself has been honored by the Southern Philippine Development Authority, the Ministry of Agriculture, the Central Bank of the Philippines, the Bureau of Forest Development and the Philippine Society of Animal Science.

Recognizing the wider application of SALT and FAITH Gardens, the Magsaysay Award Foundation named Watson the 1985 International Understanding Awardee for "encouraging international utilization of the Sloping Agricultural Land Technology created by him and his co-workers to help the poorest of small tropical farmers." Watson turned over the award monies of some P400,000 to BRLC to increase its outreach.

Learning Through Failure

Patrick James McGlinchey, SSC

Productively utilizing hitherto idle uplands is an urgent challenge for Asian agriculturalists as populations burgeon and lowlands are no longer capable of growing sufficient food. This is of particular concern in the Republic of Korea, where only one-fifth of the total land area is suitable for crops, and especially so on offshore volcanic islands like Cheju. The key to the successful development of idle wasteland, however, depends upon persuading the local peoples of the possibility and means of change.

Although Father McGlinchey went to Korea, as he has said, "to spread the Gospel of Christ," he was moved by the poverty of Cheju's 280,000 (now 500,000) inhabitants, and disturbed by the fact that over 50,000 upland hectares lay idle. But he did not intend to become personally involved. He says ruefully:

"I thought I would just make suggestions based on the many years of experience with my father in Ireland. I assumed some farmers might act on these suggestions and would as a result start generating more income. I expected other farmers to imitate the successful ones and so in due course the poverty of the small farmer would be eliminated, or at least alleviated, throughout the island. I laugh now to think how naive I was."

Patrick James McGlinchey was born on June 6, 1928 in the village of Raphoe, County Donegal, Ireland, the fifth of nine

67

children, and grew up in the town of Letterkenny. His father, Patrick McGlinchey, was a veterinary surgeon. His mother, the former Sarah O'Boyle, was a nurse.

McGlinchey attended elementary and secondary school in Letterkenny and St. Columban's College in nearby Navan. St. Columban's, the major seminary for training young men to become Columban Fathers, is not registered as a university, hence does not give degrees.

Throughout his youth McGlinchey spent his school holidays accompanying his father on his rounds, and his father's influence was profound, imbuing the boy with a concern for all aspects of an agriculturalist's struggle to wrest a living from the land. "When my father was called out on a calving case," McGlinchey recalls, "he would advise the farmer on fertilization of crops and grassland, use of pesticides, preventive medicine, marketing, government regulations and improved techniques of soil management," the very subjects McGlinchey would find himself advising Korean peasants on 20 years later.

In 1945 McGlinchey joined the Society of Saint Columban (SSC), the order whose foreign mission orientation goes back to its founder, Columban, a 6th century Irish missionary to Europe. Ordained a priest in 1951, McGlinchey was assigned the following year to the South Korean diocese of Kwangju. With the exception of this first year in Kwangju in language studies, McGlinchey has spent all his working life on the island of Cheju.

Cheju is 90 kilometers off the southern tip of the Korean peninsula, across the straits from Kyushu, Japan. With a perimeter of 194 kilometers, it is by far the largest island in South Korea. Its central feature is the now extinct volcano, Mt. Halla, whose slopes, rising 1,935 meters, are covered with rocks, forest and scrubby grass. The soil is red lava, porous, with an inability to retain water. Therefore, although the island has moderate to heavy rainfall, the central portion of the island lacks a natural permanent water supply.

When McGlinchey arrived in 1953 the island and its people were the poorest in South Korea. The population of 280,000 huddled along the seacoast in small farms averaging one-third of a hectare. Although planting two crops a year, families lived at subsistence level. They were heavily in debt to moneylenders, and the despair-suicide of children was not unknown. Yet 50,000 hectares of central land stood idle.

The people, as McGlinchey soon realized, had a "herd instinct," developed as the result of centuries of war and banditry (some 60,000 persons were killed during the 1947–49 period of communist guerilla activity alone). The desire to cling together along the coast was also, perhaps, linked to ancestor worship and a determination to remain on family lands.

McGlinchey began his ministry on the west coast in the small town of Hallim. His parish area had a population of 40,000, only 25 of whom were Catholic. Nevertheless one of his first acts was to build a stone church.

Since his arrival on Cheju coincided roughly with the end of the hostilities of the Korean War, McGlinchey found himself the dispenser of food and clothing provided by Catholic Relief Services, itself a conduit for private and governmental aid from the United States. The relief services were necessary at the time, but McGlinchey soon became convinced that continued assistance was not the answer; it would be better by far for the people to become self-sufficient.

At first, the priest says of himself, he berated the farmers for their lack of initiative, urging them to utilize the idle land, to feed and care for their chickens and pigs, and upgrade their stock. The farmers' reply was typically: "The idle land around here is no good. The only pigs or chickens or cattle or grass that will grow are the ones that you see now. It is useless and a waste of time to try to change them. Otherwise our ancestors would have done so."

His next reaction was to try to *show* the people how they could improve their lot, but in seminary he was trained in religion and philosophy, not in agriculture, and even though he had imbided a general knowledge of farmers and farming from his father, he had no practical experience. His first years of attempting to improve the agriculturalists' lot, therefore, were years of learning through failure.

McGlinchey's first project was to form a 4-H Club to promote modern farm methods and good citizenship among the youth of the parish. With his own money he imported a few purebred piglets—Duroc, Landrace, and Yorkshire. He held classes to teach the teenagers how to care for the pigs, then gave them the animals to raise, hoping thereby to upgrade the stock on their parents' farms.

To McGlinchey's great disappointment the adults refused to cooperate, turning the animals out to forage, and selling or slaughtering them when the first feast day came around. He thus learned that in Korea's Confucian society, age would not accept advice from youth. To make meaningful changes he would have to wait until these 4H Club members were themselves adults, marrying, and on farms of their own.

During the intervening four or five years he spent his spare time walking across the central wastelands to learn the terrain and try to determine how the wasteland might be utilized. As an Irish countryman he first thought of raising sheep, even though the grass was poor and short-lived. But before importing sheep he decided to set up a cottage industry to use wool from the animals already on the island so there would be an established market for fleece from the flocks he envisioned.

This was his second failure: neither he nor the island women knew enough about wool preparation and knitting to produce marketable wear. No one, he says, but his fellow Columbans bought the lumpy socks he tried to sell.

Recognizing now the need for both expertise and capital, neither of which was available in Korea, McGlinchey decided to seek both abroad while on home leave. He met with little response in the United States but persuaded MISEREOR (the German Catholic Church Social Aid Fund) and OXFAM of England, Ireland and Canada, to give help "piecemeal." He also received funds from his family and friends.

Again misfortune dogged him. With a loan from MISEREOR McGlinchey bought 500 high quality sheep and arranged for a local Catholic religious order to distribute them to Korean farmers, but supervise their feeding and care. While the sheep were enroute on the high seas, McGlinchey learned that the order was unable to meet its commitment to him and intended to keep the sheep on its own farm. Refusing to acknowledge defeat, the priest himself accepted the sheep and distributed them to willing farmers. But it was winter, the farmers had made no preparations for the sheep and McGlinchey had no fodder to give them; most of the animals died of malnutrition.

His next priority, nonetheless, was to upgrade the weaving project. While on home leave he had persuaded the Columban order to assign to Cheju several Columban Sisters who were knowledgeable in weaving, knitting and design. The project began in earnest with the arrival of the sisters in late 1962. A wool processing and weaving factory was set up in quonset huts—obtained from the U.S. Air Force Radar Station on Cheju—using second-hand machinery purchased with funds from MISEREOR. This central factory where the wool was cleaned, spun, dyed and woven into bolts of tweed, had by 1975 over 40 permanent workers. Meanwhile the knitting was done in 300 island households by the wives and daughters of farmers; the knitters averaged a sweater per week and earned about US$6 per item. These handwoven sweaters (plus scarves, caps and gloves) were sold through major hotels and department stores in Seoul and were in great demand by foreigners. They sold for a third the price of Irish handknits which they resembled. This was McGlinchey's first success.

Converting the idle lands of central Cheju into fertile pastures and farms became another success story. Starting with the purchase of two-thirds of a hectare in 1959, McGlinchey eventually bought 1,000 hectares in the central part of the island and an equal amount in scattered plots elsewhere. Farmers were glad to get rid of their idle land by selling it to "that crazy red-haired foreigner." But because of what that crazy foreigner and his colleagues did, the worth of the land increased 150 fold in 15 years. The original land purchase is the site of the training farm of the Isidore Development Association (IDA).

Called Isidore after the 13th century Spanish patron-saint of farmers, the name is fitting. Koreans pronounce it "Isidol": *isi* in Japanese means rock and *dol* is rock in Korean. Since Cheju is known to all Koreans for three things—rocks, wind and women, all traditionally in excess—nothing better identifies the land on which IDA is located than "rocky rocks."

When IDA was formally established in 1963, under the presidency of the Catholic archbishop, and with a board of directors that included three Koreans, McGlinchey was relieved of his pastoral duties to give his full time to its development.

The first venture was a central farm which later became the Central Training Farm. IDA sent a young man to the mainland for six months' training. When he returned he and several other volunteers, most of them original 4H Club members, opened up the new lands, building roads and walls and clearing the rocky soil for farming and pasturage—all without equipment.

Lack of a permanent water supply was a hurdle that had to be overcome if the land was to be made fertile. McGlinchey solved this problem by burying heavy plastic in the ground to create a reservoir of 4,000 ton capacity. The next difficulty was the grass itself. The native grass grows to about four centimeters in height during June and July; at the end of August it turns brown and the land becomes useless for grazing until the following May. McGlinchey attempted to upgrade the pasturage by importing seed from other parts of the world but he was unsuccessful in finding the right grass for the climate, soil and terrain until he also began importing foreign experts.

Today, on the advice of a young New Zealand agriculturalist, who was recruited by CORSO (the New Zealand Council of Organizations for Relief Services Overseas), a New Zealand grass grows luxuriantly on the downs of Cheju. Reaching a height of 40 cm. the grass, McGlinchey admits, is even greener and richer than that of Ireland. Two hectares will now support five healthy cows, instead of the one scrawny creature of a few years back. Sheep are brought in to graze behind the cattle, and the dung and urine of both help fertilize the land, although commercial fertilizer must be added. The sheep also help sow. In the spring they are fed seed which passes through their digestive tracts, spreads through their droppings across the fields and is tramped into the ground by their hooves.

Once he found the correct grass for the uplands McGlinchey, again with the help of CORSO, imported 600 purebred sheep from New Zealand. But again the project almost faltered because the farmers knew little about livestock raising. The venture was saved by two CORSO-supported volunteer veterinarians from Australia.

On Cheju the profit to the farmer from sheep is less than from pigs or cattle. Therefore McGlinchey again attempted pig raising in 1962 when he learned that he could obtain corn for such a project under Title II of U.S. Public Law 480. The only expense to the recipient was the cost of transportation which the Korean government agreed to pay. Catholic Relief undertook to sponsor the project to ensure its tax-free status.

With assurance of the availability of free feed McGlinchey imported the piglets, giving farmers 20 each. IDA helped the farmers build fattening houses and supplied them with the PL480 corn, on credit, at half the market price. The farmers were to be paid for the fatted pigs on the basis of the difference between their original cost plus the price of feed, and their weight value. Later McClinchey established a price for the farmer midway between the market's cyclical highs and lows—a profit of approximately US$16 per animal.

Once more the farmers failed to abide by the arrangement. They sold the corn—which was in short supply—to mainland buyers and turned the pigs loose to forage for themselves. When he discovered what was happening, McGlinchey was forced to take back the pigs and develop fattening houses on the IDA central farm.

This episode had unpleasant consequences for McGlinchey. Angry at having their lucrative, although illegal, income stopped (a provision of the feed gift by the U.S. was that it not be resold) and the piglets taken back, farmers and grain merchants began making charges of "smuggling, tax-dodging and self-enrichment" against McGlinchey to Korean and American authorities and the press. The priest endured 14 months of public and private harassment until the accusations finally ceased; both the authorities and the people realized they were baseless.

The central farm, of necessity, developed both breeding and fattening houses. Pregnant sows were kept tied—an innovation in Korea—to prevent them from fighting, and were yoked after giving birth to prevent them from rolling over on their young. Modern equipment was installed which allowed one farmer to feed the pigs and clean their stalls simultaneously, enabling him to handle 279 sows in 20 minutes. The piglets were fattened to 95 pounds before being slaughtered for meat. Importing a total of 1,500 pigs, in three years IDA was selling that many fatted animals per month to Japanese buyers. As a result of its proven success IDA was able to reinstitute the animal boarding system, assured that farmers would now feed the piglets with the IDA-provided feed.

When PL480 corn was discontinued in 1972 (the U.S. having concluded that Korea was now able to feed itself), and the cost of feed tripled, McGlinchey looked around for other fodder. He found that the local sweet potato alcohol factory was polluting the sea with its residue. Devising a method for separating the solids from the liquid, he persuaded the company to give him the solid waste in return for extracting it from system. As a result he obtained a ton of dry matter suitable for fodder from every two tons of residue he hauled to the IDA feed mill for processing. The mill, where the residue is mixed with protein concentrate, was financed by the earlier PL480 corn sale. Pigs "loved" the new food but fattened on it more slowly—in eight to nine months instead of six. Nevertheless the cost of fattening them was nominal.

Selling the meat on a wider and permanent scale became the next priority. McGlinchey visited Japan and Hong Kong to check market possibilities; he became the first in Korea to sell frozen meat to Japan, signing an agreement with a Japanese importer to provide frozen boned pork on a monthly basis. To do so he converted an unused fish freezing plant on the east coast into a frozen meat plant, but the distance—seven and a half miles by difficult roads—forced him to build a new plant near the IDA farm.

The IDA example was followed by others on the mainland and by 1975 the export of frozen meat to Japan was a US$12 million business, with IDA accounting for US$1 million. The market continued to expand and McGlinchey began a weekly radio program urging farmers to raise pigs.

As more farmers began to raise pigs, and IDA's training program expanded, middlemen began playing IDA against the small farmers in order to force down prices. This caused financial loss and bad feelings among the farmers.

McGlinchey thus learned another lesson—that the agent of change should not remain involved once the intended benefactor has mastered the necessary techniques. He therefore stopped raising pigs in 1979 and sold the herd of—by then—12,000 pigs to staff members who had been in charge of the animals. He also rented them the pig-houses and helped them and the other local farmers organize a cooperative. The cooperative reduced the number of pigs to meet the level of demand and stabilized prices.

Since the objective of IDA was to improve the incomes of farmers by teaching them productive farming and livestock techniques, the central farm was organized as a training center where a young farmer could live, learn by doing and be paid on the basis of his results. The training period was originally six months but was soon extended to a minimum of one year. A farmer could bring his wife and one or two children to live in the simple housing which was built with a grant from CORSO. Seventy or 80 families could be accommodated.

Only agriculturalists trained at IDA were eligible to buy the pure breed animals imported or bred on the farm, and they had to agree to use IDA feed which was specifically designed for optimum results. Religion had nothing to do with acceptance at IDA. Trainees did not even have to be residents of Cheju; by 1975 one-third of the trainees were from the mainland. Those trained at IDA could also obtain credit assistance to buy house, land, livestock and feed. They were required to contribute 50 percent of the operating capital; after three years' grace they were given ten years in which to repay the balance at three and one-half percent interest.

The housing units were a first for Korea. They were constructed in the form of the ancient Ctesiphon arch, which is "⅔ as high as it is wide, with curved, thin cement roof joining the foundation while serving as a wall." This design had been adapted over the centuries by Irish and English engineers; McGlinchey himself had built three Ctesiphon arch houses in Ireland. The design proved its worth on Cheju during the typhoon of 1972, when buildings so constructed remained intact, while other buildings suffered severe damage.

The IDA-trained farmers have a dual incentive for repaying the loans that make their farm ownership possible. Twice the amount they repay is deposited in their credit union and they can borrow this sum, provided three-fourths of the loan is for productive investment. There have been problems, nevertheless, in policing the expenditure of funds.

In 1973 McGlinchey began a new livestock venture, breeding cattle, a project that doubled in size while still in the planning stage. McGlinchey decided to import 450 Hereford cattle from Australia to upgrade the stock on Cheju and MISEREOR agreed to pay 75 percent of the cost. Economics of scale, however, caused the Australian exporters to refuse to ship fewer than 1,000 head. Therefore McGlinchey had to persuade others to take 300 and had to accept the remaining 250 himself. Consequently 961 pregnant Hereford cows and 39 bulls were shipped to Cheju. At the same time McGlinchey signed an agreement with Japanese meat importers who guaranteed to purchase 500 grain-fattened beef cattle per month once the project was underway.

The cattle were off-loaded from a German cattle transport onto barges in the open sea in December 1973. Both barges and personnel were lent by the U.S. Army Port Operations-Pusan; the difficult job was accomplished without a hitch. Three days of perfect weather and a glassy sea—extraordinary conditions, particularly in mid-winter—simplified the task.

A second shipment of cattle was received in the summer. Possessing a total of 2,000 purebred cattle—Herefords with a few Santa Gertrudis and Brahman bulls for breeding—IDA next year was able to distribute 1,000 calves to farmers for fattening before shipping them to Japan as beef. A four-year program was also undertaken to train some 1,500 farmers to become cattlemen. The government of Korea supported the project, allocating US$1,500,000 for the program in its Third Five Year Plan.

In preparation for the original cattle shipment, silos were built to store the rich grasses growing on IDA lands, and dipping tanks—to rid the animals of ticks that infested the area—were constructed. These innovations were soon adopted in other parts of Korea. Concurrently IDA signed agreements with villages to improve their communal pasture lands by replanting them with the New Zealand grass. As the project prospered McGlinchey added a cheese factory and later a liquid-milk packing plant; In 1989 he planned to import 500 pedigreed Friesian cows to improve the island dairy industry.

As McGlinchey hoped, IDA has served as a development model. When the local farmers finally became convinced that the uplands could be cultivated and that livestock raising was profitable, they themselves began to pressure the local government to supply the necessary infrastructure. A large scale piped-water project was undertaken by the local government after McGlinchey proved it could be done; reservoirs were built and roads were improved and extended around the island.

In the mid-1970s the national government turned its attention to agriculture—after neglecting it for some years in favor of industry—and adopted many of the ideas pioneered on Cheju. It actively supported the 4-H movement and promoted the formation of 4H clubs throughout the country. It began growing New Zealand grass in other regions; importing sheep and cattle; and giving livestock loans to farmers through government cooperatives. The government also bought idle land and redistributed it to farmers on the pattern developed at IDA. Lastly, it supported the credit union movement—a movement similar to that which McGlinchey started on Cheju in 1962.

Since 1972, after a senior government official paid a surprise visit to Cheju, McGlinchey has been a minor national celebrity. That year President Park Chung Hee bestowed on the priest the Order of Industrial Service Merit, Stone Tower, "in recognition of his contribution towards helping promote the nation's livestock industry," and asked him to address the Economic Planning Board to discuss IDA projects. The government also produced a half hour documentary television film of his work entitled, "The Sheep and Pig Farmer," which it showed nationwide.

McGlinchey contributed the money which accompanied the award (US$1,850) to the IDA clinic which the Columban Sisters had started in 1970. The clinic has expanded to include the St. Isidore Home for the Destitute (1981), which cares for the blind, the handicapped, and the elderly who have been abandoned by their families. This was followed by the St. Isidore Day-Care Center for the Aged, and the St. Isidore School for the Elderly, plus more traditional kindergartens and day-care centers for children.

Most recently McGlinchey has set up a new organization

designed to encourage Catholics all over Cheju to work with the old and to adopt them as "foster grannies and granddaddies," taking them into their own homes. The object of the program is eventually to eliminate the need for institutional care. A realist, he accepts the fact that the program will probably grow slowly; it takes time for such a revolutionary idea to be accepted. To encourage participation, however, McGlinchey has built 20 new houses at IDA for families who agree in advance to accept one or more of the needy elderly as part of their family.

Over the past 36 years McGlinchey has found the Koreans surprisingly like the Irish. Among other things, he says, both are "of generally friendly disposition, do a great deal of singing and consume considerable quantities of alcoholic beverages." In consequence of the latter he has launched "Pioneers," an Irish organization whose object is to reduce, and if possible eliminate, alcohol abuse which he finds destroying many families. This project, too, he expects will take a long time to become accepted.

Much of the progress at IDA, McGlinchey modestly says, is the result of the volunteer work of foreign experts: "amateur do-gooders" are bold enough to try unlikely new projects, but professionals, he insists, are needed to bring them to fruition. In recognition of this approach McGlinchey received the 1975 Ramon Magsaysay Award in International Understanding for "mobilizing international support and foreign volunteers to modernize livestock farming in his adopted country."

Volunteers have come to IDA from the Irish Columban Fathers and Sisters, from the Voluntary Missionary Movement in London, and through CORSO. Many had farm experience or were graduates of agricultural colleges. The New Zealand and Australian volunteers, all graduates of agricultural colleges, stayed for at least two years, one extending his stay to four. Volunteers paid their own expenses, with IDA paying their transportation costs through a grant from OXFAM. The volunteers lived in housing provided at the Isidore Farm and worked with both the farm staff and local farmers. Experience taught McGlinchey that the foreign workers should be regarded as volunteers only, without authority over the Korean staff.

The list of international donors that McGlinchey has persuaded to assist development on Cheju is lengthy. Ireland's Gorta (Gaelic for hunger) has been generous to IDA, providing farm equipment, prefabricated cattle sheds (these proved cheaper to import from Ireland than build in Korea) and veterinary medicine. OXFAM supported numerous projects: e.g., the installation of 16 kilometers of water pipe; electricity for the farm; farm equipment; housing for pigs, and a garage, machine shop and mobile clinic. It also absorbed the travel and housing expenses of the foreign technical staff. OXFAM and Gorta together made possible the purchase of Ford tractors which were built especially for use on slopes and were the first of their kind in Korea; Ford later opened a plant to assemble them there.

MISEREOR, in turn, provided the first funds—other than the US$5,000 given by McGlinchey's own family—to purchase land for the Idle Lands Development Project. Over the years it has made grants and loans for the spinning and weaving factory in Hallim, the IDA clinic, the importation of sheep and cattle, the travel expenses of foreign technical experts and the farm training projects. Catholic Relief Services made possible the procurement of PL480 corn for the hog project whose profits went to develop the resettlement program, and was the conduit through which material and equipment were imported into Korea tax free. CORSO supplied funds for the construction of schoolrooms, office, dining hall and quarters for the trainees.

Today, McGlinchey recognizes, South Korea's vibrant and growing economy no longer qualifies it for international aid, yet rural development has not kept pace with industrialization. During the decade of the nineties he urges the government and the professionals to assume the risks necessary to modernize and increase the productivity and income-generating capabilities of the rural economy.

To show what can be accomplished he points out that by the end of 1987 IDA had created new jobs for 1,000 people on Cheju and generated increased income for thousands more. If loan capital is made available at reasonable rates by international aid organizations, McGlinchey is convinced that he can double or treble these figures. However, if neither the Korean government nor international development agencies are willing to assume responsibility, McGlinchey is prepared to continue in his self-

assumed role of initiator and fund raiser—still willing to learn
by failure if necessary. Christians, he believes, "have to work
for their neighbors," and his neighbors are those who are near
him, wherever he is.

The Scientific Approach

Jiro Kawakita

Nepal, an independent land-locked kingdom, is surrounded on three sides by India, and on the northeast by China (Tibet) and the high Himalayas. Its precipitous hillsides and narrow valleys are today threatened by deforestation, soil erosion and resultant landslides. Nevertheless 90 percent of its people rely upon agriculture for a livelihood.

More than 30 years ago Jiro Kawakita began studying the disintegrating environmental equilibrium of the Sikha Valley, a once self-sufficient valley four days' walk from Pokhara. The area was faced with population growth and pressure on limited land, and hillsides and forests were being destroyed as need for livestock forage compelled larger and ever-higher hillside fields.

Kawakita understood the needs of the area, but his method of addressing them was to persuade the villagers to enunciate their own perceptions of these needs. In so doing he developed a sense of mutual participation between himself and the villagers based on a common understanding of the ecological and cultural environment. At the same time he encouraged Japan, a nation that had previously been a receiver rather than a donor, to embrace the concept of international technological assistance.

Jiro Kawakita was born on May 11, 1920, the fourth of six children and second son of banker Kyudayu Kawakita and his wife Tame Ito. Shortly after his birth in Tsu City, near Kyoto, the family moved to Tokyo, but returned to Kyoto after the devastating Kanto earthquake of 1923. By the end of primary school Kawakita had already exhibited scientific inclinations, collecting plants and insects, and showing a keen interest in chemistry. In First Middle School he joined a mountaineering club, thus embarking upon a pastime that would eventually take him from the hills around Kyoto to the Himalayas of Nepal.

Kawakita's intellectual interests deepened during the next few years. He read the works of major Western and Eastern philosophers and was attracted in particular to the writings of Henri Louis Bergson (French) and Kitaro Nishida (Japanese), both of whom emphasized the importance of direct perception and human inspiration rather than strict logic. Under the influence of these thinkers Kawakita's interests shifted away from analytical science toward a broader, more complicated perspective which encompassed the chaos or specificity of real life—the recognition that people, places and conditions do not lend themselves to neat generalizations.

In high school Kawakita therefore studied geography, a science he found "more complicated" than chemistry. During four of the next five summers he joined expeditions for geographical and ecological research on the Bonin, Volcano, Mariana, Marshall and Caroline islands of the Pacific, and in the Great Khingang Range of Manchuria.

At Kyoto Imperial University the young student became interested in the writings of the American geographer Isaiah Bowman, particularly his book entitled *The Pioneer Fringe of the New World*. As a result of his own experiences in the "pioneer fringes" of Asia, Kawakita gradually expanded his field of interest to include cultural anthropology. On the basis of research during the two Manchurian expeditions in which he participated he wrote his university thesis on "Land Reclamation of the Northeast Asian Countries."

World War II shortened his university stay to two and a half years. Conscripted as an infantryman into the Japanese Army he did not see action, for by that time the seas around Japan were infested with American submarines and his unit was unable to join the rest of his regiment in South China. Nevertheless the trauma of war made the young geographer, who was blessed with a sensitive heart as well as an inquiring mind, determined to devote his skills to the global, rather than the purely national, community. He vowed to contribute to the cause of peace by helping underdeveloped societies achieve economic wellbeing because he perceived that population and economic pressures were the frequent causes of conflict.

When the war was over Kawakita became a part-time researcher at the Kihara Institute for Biological Research and was sent to supervise the institute's farm in Tottori Prefecture at the foot of Mt. Daisan. Although he spent only 10 months with the institute, his interest in agricultural management was awakened and he benefited from his study of the remote villages in the northern mountains. As he learned more about land productivity and the population capacity of land under various conditions, he began to develop the ideas on land and population that he had first explored at the university, and evolved a scientific system to determine the population capacity of the habitable world, based on calculation of the annual calorie production on any given agricultural field. His system eliminates the problem of what crop is grown—e.g. whether the staple is rice, wheat or corn—or in which part of the world. Having calculated the average productivity of a particular piece of land, he can then calculate its population capacity. He published this methodology in its final form in 1949.

The year 1953 was to change Kawakita's life. In that year the Japan Alpine Club sent a major expedition to Nepal to climb the unscaled 8,156 meter high Mt. Manaslu. Attached to this party was a two-man scientific research team that included Kawakita, then a professor at the Institute of Geography of Osaka City University. While climbers scaled the peak Kawakita (March to August) studied the region's plant ecology and ethnogeography and learned to love the mountain people. He produced three research papers from this expedition—"Vegetation," "Crop Zone" and "Ethnogeographical Observations on the Nepal Himalaya"—all of which appeared in the two volume report, *Scientific Results of the Japanese Expedition to Nepal Himalaya 1952–1953.*

Five years later Kawakita himself organized a second, purely scientific, expedition to Nepal which was composed of academics from a number of different institutions. It was sponsored by the Japanese Society of Ethnology and the Fauna and Flora Research Society of Kyoto University, and financed, for the most part, by Japanese corporations.

After climbing Mukut Himal, the team conducted ethnogeographic, agricultural and botanical research in the Dolpo district north of the Dhaulagiri Mountains. During this trip Kawakita's affection for the remote areas of that country became deeper, and he determined that in the future he would carry out some small-scale technological project "for this beloved land"—despite the risks to his academic career of spending his time in the practical application of his ideas.

In April 1960 Kawakita was appointed to the faculty of the Department of Polytechnics, Tokyo Institute of Technology. Three years later he led an expedition, sponsored again by the Japanese Society of Ethnology, to study the culture of rice-cultivating peoples in Southeast Asia, and was finally able to lay the foundation for the program he hoped to develop of technological cooperation with the mountain people of Nepal. The team conducted part of its ethnogeographical research in a group of villages in the Dhaulagiri zone, in particular in an area Kawakita named the Sikha Valley after one of its villages; the valley had no name.

The Sikha Valley lies on the southwest side of Mt. Annapurna 1, one of Nepal's highest peaks. Of the five villages clinging to the valley's slopes, four are inhabited predominantly by Magars and are situated between 1,800 and 2,200 meters above sea level, near the upper limits of cultivation. Culturally they lie between the lowland areas of Hindu civilization and the highland areas of Tibetan civilization. Consequently they have what Kawakita terms a "two-layered culture," holding to various tribal religions, yet at the same time adopting elements from Hinduism and Tibetan Buddhism. In both the Hindu and Tibetan cultures societal units consist of a group of villages, but in the intermediate zone of the two-layered culture each village is self-contained and thus offered Kawakita small, discrete societies with which to work.

The villagers of the Sikha Valley cultivate primarily wheat, barley, corn and millet on small terraces carved out of the mountain, and pasture their water buffalo, cows, sheep and goats in the *jangal* (forests) and alpine grasslands above. The animals provide among other things, the manure which is essential to the fertility of the fields.

Kawakita's research in 1963 suggested that the Sikha Valley "was experiencing an ecological disaster of major proportions." Unprecedented population growth over the past century (over 500 percent in Sikha Village, which had grown from 60 to 325 households) had caused the people to cut down the forests for new crop and pasture land, thus setting in motion a vicious cycle. Deforestation of the hillsides was causing landslides and soil erosion. At the same time the productivity of the land in use had deteriorated, creating the need for more land-clearing, which in turn caused further deterioration. The decrease in income resulting from degradation of the land had forced many people to emigrate to the cities. Emigration meant fewer hands to take the cattle to the ever higher summer pastures. Consequently fewer animals were raised, producing less manure to fertilize the fields, which in turn led to a further decrease in land productivity.

Moreover, since forage was no longer within easy reach of the villagers, fewer animals could be maintained through the winter; by the same token, the closest forest areas were overcut for both forage and firewood. The depletion of vegetation also caused some of the nearby water sources to dry up, and the limited water supply meant not only a lower crop yield and resultant lower income, but increased health problems and a general decrease in the quality of personal and community life.

Kawakita sought solutions to these problems through a method of research, soon to be known throughout Japan as the KJ (Kawakita, Jiro) Method, that sorted and assimilated enormous quantities of purely qualitative data. He had begun to develop this methodology as early as 1951 when standard anthropological field techniques seemed to him inadequate.

At that time he had determined that analytical studies of environment, population, kinship, village organization and religious beliefs were of secondary importance to the study of their *interrelationships*. In the same way statistical analyses that dealt with the simple ratio between population and natural resources told him little he wanted to know. These so-called scientific methods, he points out, "neglect the holistic integration of qualitative data," the study of the total ecology: they attempt to fit facts into predetermined, generalized categories, failing to recognize—what Kawakita considers of primary importance— that each area and its problems are idiosyncratic and must be treated as such.

The problem facing Kawakita was how to draw conclusions from the chaotic input of the myriad of facts obtained from both objective and subjective sources. His fundamental premise, as he set about this task, was to "let the facts speak for themselves," rather than impose any preconceived ideas or hypotheses upon them. Thus he started by writing down in sentence form, on individual labels, each item of datum. He then collated the labels according to the relationships he perceived among them. Each group was given a title, usually a short sentence exactly describing the perceived relationship. Additional relationships were sought among the groupings themselves, until the entire body of facts was reduced to a manageable number of headings. Through subsequent experience Kawakita concluded the number of headings should be 10 or less for the overall view to be easily understood and a consensus achieved.

His research convinced Kawakita that many of the villagers' basic needs could be met with two innovations that were within the scope of a small technological cooperation project. These were ropelines to facilitate the transportation of fodder, firewood and manure down the mountainside; and pipelines to bring clean water into the villages.

The people of the valley knew how to dig waterways on the side of the mountain but such channels, cut into the soft layers of schist, induced mudslides that quickly destroyed them. Pipelines, laid on the ground, would preserve the fragile geological structure and reduce the incidence of slides. The valley enjoys a moderate climate so freezing posed no problem.

Although Kawakita was confident these two innovations were the solution to the key problems of the villagers, he recognized the necessity of testing whether the villagers perceived the priority of the problems as he did. If so, did they perceive the pipeline and the ropeline as the most suitable solutions, and would they participate in their installation? Rather than resort to the anthropologist's classic use of carefully prepared questionnaires, he chose to chat with the people around the fire, night after night, mixing suggestions with gossip and refraining from persuasion.

This process he calls the Key Problem Approach. Because it included a high degree of villager input at all levels, it proved extremely effective in developing consensus among the villagers regarding both priorities and solutions. Concensus, in turn, promoted a high degree of motivation, which Kawakita felt was the vital force necessary for the achievement of the project.

He knew, from the outset, that the KJ Method and the Key Problem Approach had far wider application than the Sikha Valley Project. This was borne out by the immediate popularity of the booklet he published on his return to Japan in 1964 called *Patigaku* (Partyship), which applied the KJ Method to aspects of business such as leadership and partnership. The many requests he received to teach the method led to its further refinement and eventually to his publication of a new book three years later entitled *Hasso-ho* (Method of Idea Generation). Interest in the course spread from middle level businessmen to other levels of the business sector, and soon gained popularity among university students and researchers.

Back in Japan Kawakita had also attended to the practical aspects of the Sikha Valley Project. After some study he and his students settled on polyvinyl chloride (PVC) as the best material for the water pipeline. As to the ropeline, they realized that, although the ropeline technology was not difficult, a special type of wire would have to be developed to suit the specific conditions of the Sikha Valley. The rope needed to be light in weight as it had to be transported up the mountain by foot. It must also have very high tensile strength since the geography of the valley required each span to be quite long. Finally the rope must be very durable because the people of the valley were poor and could not afford frequent replacements. To create such a rope Kawakita turned to the research department of the Shinko Kosen Company, a subsidiary of Kobe Steel, which produced a 6-millimeter wire rope fitting his specifications.

Kawakita had a philosophic as well as a practical reason for demanding an "advanced technology ropeline"—something not yet required by the developed world. He firmly believes that unless underdeveloped communities are given advanced technologies to solve traditional problems they will always be at a disadvantage vis-a-vis advanced communities, even those within their own country. And they need both new and interlocking technologies (e.g. the ropeline *and* the pipeline) to build upon in order to achieve the quality of life they seek.

Funding proved more difficult than technology. Although his project proposal was well received by both the Nepalese and Japanese governments, "the bureaucratic obstacles involved in going through official channels proved too numerous," and Kawakita decided instead to seek financing from the private sector.

Having made this decision, however, he had to shelve the project temporarily. The wave of student unrest at Japanese universities in 1969 struck Tokyo Institute of Technology, causing great turmoil among both students and faculty. Kawakita himself felt the students were wrong in the way they proceeded and "couldn't accept their way of thinking," but he disagreed strongly with the university's management of the situation. In 1970 he tendered his resignation.

Having separated himself from a formal educational institution, yet needing to support himself, his wife and infant son, Kawakita embarked upon an experimental educational alternative which he called Ido Daigaku, or Mobile University. It consisted of 17 or 18 annual two-week courses devoted to the study of environmental and ecological problems. The courses were held in various parts of Japan and were site-related. In each course students were divided into three units made up of six teams. In Shiga Prefecture, for example, Kawakita asked the units to study how to make the wisest use of Lake Biwa. Under this general direction each team selected a particular sub-theme. Meanwhile Kawakita founded the Kawakita Research Institute in Tokyo (1970) for the purpose of disseminating the KJ Method.

Throughout this period of personal and professional transition and experimentation Kawakita did not lose sight of the proposed Sikha Valley Project. With limited funds, and realizing that any new technology should be first tested on a small scale, Kawakita persuaded four members of the Tokyo Institute of Technology Alpine Club to do some experimental work for him in the Sikha Valley (in 1970) after they had completed a climbing expedition. During the course of their work they constructed 1,000 meters of pipeline and 500 meters of ropeway.

The results were mixed but they provided valuable information for the later full-scale project. The ropeway, constructed as a two-way system, proved too short for the valley's needs. Moreover the villagers, it developed, required only a *downhill* line; the fuel and fodder baskets when empty were so light that the number required could be carried uphill by a single person. The need for the ropeway was to transport the filled carriers *down* into the valley.

The pipeline, on the other hand, proved so successful that when Kawakita went to the valley four years later to inaugurate the main project, he found the Nepalese government, in cooperation with UNICEF, had already adopted the idea and had begun to build pipelines in a number of other mountain villages. Today the pipeline is a major USAID-supported project for bringing clean water to Nepalese villages.

In the meantime a second reconnaissance party reaffirmed the willingness of the villagers to push ahead with the projects. Kawakita at this point formally organized a private, non-profit volunteer organization called ATCHA (Association for Technical Cooperation to the Himalayan Areas), whose acronym means "fine" in Hindi. Its broad purpose is to discover the main needs, and the optimum technology for meeting them, of villages in underdeveloped rural areas, especially those in mountainous terrain.

ATCHA seeks to achieve its goals through a combined program of research and technological adaptation, with participation by the beneficiaries at all stages of the project. Kawakita believes that small-scale volunteer projects can serve the people of an underdeveloped area better than the bureaucratically designed projects of government and corporate business that construct major dams and road systems, but do little if anything to ensure that the quality of life of the people they serve is enhanced. Through ATCHA he also hopes to develop the spirit of volunteerism in Japan. The board of ATCHA, headed by Kawakita, is composed of notable Japanese intellectuals.

In the autumn of 1974 a long cavalcade, headed by Kawakita on horseback, wended its way for four days from the airstrip of Pokhara into the deep Himalayas. Behind him was a team of some 10 backpacking Japanese engineers, followed by a long string of Magars, each laden with a coil of rope or a section of PVC pipe. The party also included Hideaki Miyazawa, the Japanese inventor of the modern hydraulic ram.

The hydraulic ram is traceable to the 19th century water hammer that used the pressure of the water flow itself to lift a running stream from a lower to a higher elevation. By mixing air bubbles with the water, Miyazawa was able to develop a pump that could lift water 120–200 meters, using only the natural pressure of water dropping 30 meters (vertically 4 meters). ATCHA had decided to test this technology in the Sikha Valley.

The ropeline to be installed this time was designed for down-hill use only and consisted of spans of more than 1,000 meters each. The villagers welcomed the new ropeline with great enthu-siasm, which seemed to Kawakita proof enough that it met their true needs. By the end of May 1975 the group had installed nine kilometers of ropeline, four kilometers of pipeline and two hydraulic rams for the use of three villages.

A follow-up study in 1977 revealed some technical difficulties occurring in the pipeline systems, particularly in the water tanks into which the pipes emptied and in the hydraulic rams. Also some of the springs had become polluted because of the in-creased number of livestock grazing nearby. But there were no further problems with the ropelines.

In the case of the rams, the pressure of the water proved so strong that its constant surge broke the major valve. Kawakita attributes the water project problems, not to careless manage-ment by the villagers, but to the careless mistakes of the instal-lation team and poor quality-control by one manufacturer. More-over, the members of the water project team were not experts in pipeline or natural force pump technology, whereas the ropeline team had included a few specialists.

The team investigated charges that, with increased accessibil-ity to the forests via the ropeline, overcutting would be greatly accelerated. It found, however, "no evidence that the ropelines had or would accelerate the destruction of forests, both in the view of the villagers as well as in that of the team." In fact the villagers saw the ropeline as a way to protect the *jangals*— towards which they had always had an almost religious attitude, recognizing them as a source of great benefits: they had abused them only out of economic necessity. The ropeline, by cutting down tremendously on the time involved in transport, enabled the villagers to range further afield and cut more selectively; they had even found time for some minor reforestation. The most important cause of the degradation of the forest was not overcutting, but overgrazing, the team report stated, a condition not influenced by the ropeline.

Despite problems, Kawakita feels that the impact of the project has been good and its influence has spread beyond the confines of the villages concerned. The most remarkable result is a new spirit of self-reliance, fostered, he believes, by the "personal participation" method his group used in developing and implementing the program. Infected by the success of the Sikha Valley experiment a large number of villages in the western hills of Nepal were encouraged to improve their own communities.

In March 1978 Kawakita was invited to join the faculty of Tsukuba University. Within the Tsukuba area are concentrated the major research and development institutions of Japan. Kawakita was appointed Professor of Cultural Anthropology in the Institute of History and Anthropology, and Professor of Cultural Ecology in the Graduate School of Environmental Science. That same year he received the Prince Chichibu Memorial Academic Prize, given by the Japan Society for the Promotion of Science, in recognition of his research for his English language book, *The Hill Magars and Their Neighbours*. In September the King of Nepal decorated him for his research and projects in Nepal, and for his role in developing cultural interchange between Japan and Nepal.

Under Kawakita's direction in August 1979 ATCHA began a series of studies in the still primitive hill villages of Akka, in northern Japan. The group compared the cultural ecology of the Akkan area with that of the Himalayan. Using the same principle of village participation ATCHA developed successful projects in 13 mountain villages.

One of the devices that proved successful in the Akka region was tested in Nepal in 1982 and 1983 when ATCHA was invited to return to extend the ropeline system. The team took with it a boat designed to cross powerful mountain torrents, utilizing only the force of the stream's current.

The need for such a ferry had become evident to the villagers as well as to ATCHA. In former days, when each community was self-sufficient, crossing rivers was not as essential to the people's socio-economic wellbeing as it is in today's exchange economy. Beginning in 1952 the Swiss Association for Technical Assistance and the Nepalese government had constructed hanging bridges across river chasms, but by the 1980s construction costs had skyrocketed. A less expensive technolgoy was therefore called for.

Kawakita had asked the Tokyo Institute of Technology to design a suitable stream-powered ferryboat for Akka. The institute had produced a simple lightweight craft that was propelled by a rope attached to the shore and, in a Y configuration, to the sides of the boat. The boatman could manipulate the angle of the rope so that the current would push the vessel from one shore to the other. The model which Kawakita took to Nepal was an air-filled rubber dinghy which proved suitable to the needs of the Nepalese mountain people. ATCHA has since designed a lightweight but sturdy fiber-reinforced plastic that can be used for on-the-spot construction of such ferryboats, sized according to the needs of a particular location. The building technique is simple enough for the local people to learn.

Anticipating the future, Kawakita also asked the institute to construct a boat that could travel *upstream* against powerful mountain currents, using those currents for power. The institute devised a system using a 1-to-3 kilometer length of rope attached to the shore, but following the course of the river, and a boat designed with a paddlewheel, *against* which the water pushes to help move the vehicle upstream. The adoption of these boat-ropelines will enable the mountain people to utilize otherwise impassable rivers for transportation.

In recent years the disastrous ecological situation of the Nepal Himalayas has received extensive international attention. In consequence the United Nations established a new organization in Nepal for the protection and development of the entire Himalayan area. The International Center for Integrated Mountain Development, as it is titled, requested Kawakita to organize a support group of interested Japanese scientists. The result is the Japan Scientific Cooperation Center for the Mountain Area, founded in October 1983. Its members are specialists in a wide variety of fields and all of them have had experience in the Himalayas. Kawakita expects widespread results from this organization because it has opened lines of communication *within* the Japanese scientific community.

Under the auspices of ATCHA Kawakita has also organized Mountain Ecology Seminars (MES), the first of which met in Tokyo in 1985. Eighty Japanese specialist-volunteers participated. From among them 40 were recruited, trained, and at the request of the villagers and under Kawakita's leadership, visited the Sikha Valley in December–January 1985–86. Some of the specialists returned a year later to engage in a further exchange of ideas and profer additional technolgoical assistance.

Kawakita, as President of the Japan Nepal Society, helped organize the Japanese Committee of the King Mahendra Trust for Nature Conservation—which was established on the initiative of the King of Nepal to address and resolve environmental problems in the Nepalese Himalayas. Kawakita is also the first president of the Japan Creativity Society, which involves scholars, engineers, and businessmen in a variety of fields who are seeking an interdisciplinary approach to problem-solving. Kawakita firmly believes that such research into the development of human creativity is essential to the future of mankind.

With some 60 major scientific articles and books to his credit, this ever practical scholar-visionary retired in 1984 from Tsukuba University and joined the faculty of Chubu University as Professor of International Relations. That same year he received the Ramon Magsaysay Award in International Understanding for "winning the participation of remote Nepalese villagers in researching their problems, resulting in practical benefits of potable water supplies and rapid ropeway transport across mountain gorges." This "participation," Kawakita is quick to point out, is based on a common understanding of the ecological and cultural environment and its needs.

Simple Technologies

Anton Soedjarwo

In parts of Central Java, with a dry season frequently lasting five months, water is a major concern. At the end of four months farmers and their wives are often reduced to squeezing liquid from banana stalks, or walking five to ten kilometers daily to draw water from often stagnant ponds. It was such a situation that Anton Soedjarwo began to address when he was an engineering student at Gajah Mada University. Quickly recognizing that government alone cannot be responsible for rural development, he and three colleagues began their lifelong role as "activators," initiators showing rural peoples how to improve their economic lives.

The first of seven children (four boys and three girls) of Sutanto, a Chinese-Indonesian batik merchant, and his wife Suhartini, Anton Soedjarwo was born October 20, 1948 in Pekalongan, on the north coast of Central Java, in the new Republic of Indonesia. Neither Anton nor Soedjarwo was his name at birth. In Indonesia it was not yet the custom to have surnames, and his childhood name was Hian. When he was confirmed in the Catholic Church at age 10 he received the name Antonius, shortened by his friends to Anton—the given name he prefers. Later, when surnames names came into use, with the approval of his younger brothers and sisters, Anton chose the family name Soedjarwo, meaning good.

Since the family was Catholic Soedjarwo attended church schools: Pius Primary and Middle schools in Pekalongan, and Loyola High School Seminary in Semarang, graduating from the latter in 1965. During semester breaks his father took him hiking in remote areas of the country. At the time he would have preferred to spend his holidays in Jakarta or other urban surroundings but he recognizes that his feeling for rural life began with these excursions.

Because of the turmoil resulting from the September 1965 attempted communist coup in Indonesia, schools were closed for a year. Therefore it was 1966 when he enrolled at Gajah Mada University in Yogyakarta to prepare for a career in civil engineering. He completed the usual three year pre-engineering course for a bachelor's degree in only two and a half years, even though he worked to pay his tuition by playing the guitar in a local club and by writing study pamphlets. The study guides sold well, not only in Yogyakarta but in other university towns, since most students found the English-language engineering textbooks difficult to understand.

After receiving his B.A. in 1968 Soedjarwo continued engineering studies at Gajah Mada, at the same time teaching four hours a week at Atmajaya Catholic University. During this period he lived in a hostel run by a Swiss Jesuit priest, Johannes Casutt. Father Casutt, knowing that Soedjarwo and several other students were looking for a meaningful way to spend their vacations, challenged the young Indonesians to go to the villages and help their people. He offered them funds he had obtained from the International Confederation of Catholic Charities when he was in Europe on leave. The students accepted the challenge.

For their initial project they chose Turgo, a village on the slopes of volcanic Mt. Merapi, slightly northeast of Yogyakarta. Since the European system of education was in effect, and graduate students were not required to attend classes but only to pass the final examinations, the students were able to live in the village several months, long enough to understand the people's way of life and to assess their needs.

The people of Turgo were very poor. They lived in an arid

region and had to survive three to six months of the year without rain. They also had to contend with the occasional loss of homes and crops as a result of volcanic activity. To add to their woes, the isolation of the area made it an ideal hiding place for bandits and remnants of the outlawed communist party.

As many of the peasants had to spend five or six hours each day fetching water the students' first activity was to use their simple engineering skills to install a gravity-flow system of bamboo pipes to bring water to the village from a source several kilometers away.

This experience in the village, and insight into the stark reality of rural poverty, had a profound effect on Soedjarwo. He became convinced he should devote his engineering talents to rural development, even though it was a far from prestigious or profitable aspect of the profession. Moreover, the curriculum of the university, geared as it was to major construction projects, had not taught him how to work in the villages and develop simple, easily transferable technologies. Nonetheless the young student received encouragement from three persons whose approval was sufficient to counteract the social and educational environment.

The first was Father Casutt who had encouraged him in the beginning. The second was Professor Hardjoso Prodjopangarso who had visited Turgo, advising the students and assuring them that what they were doing was truly worthwhile. The third was his father, to whom he confided his plans with some trepidation, knowing that most middle class families wanted their sons to enter a profession where they could achieve social status and economic security. Fortunately, Soedjarwo's father was not an average middle class parent. He immediately encouraged his son's aspirations and assured him that, as long as he gave of himself wholeheartedly, his work would be meaningful and fruitful.

The following year (1969) Soedjarwo and his colleagues started a water project in the village of Ngembesan and in 1970 they undertook a program in the Cankringan district. The latter was a large project, involving 50 villages and 32,000 people, and took the volunteers and villagers more than a year and a half to complete. The work was not without danger since it involved raising water over precipitous terrain from a ravine 200 meters deep. Six to seven hundred villagers were mobilized daily to cut and lay bamboo pipes. When dynamite had to be used to cut through rock, Soedjarwo set the charge himself. In one instance he pushed the detonator and no explosion occurred. Motioning the others to stay back he investigated and found the fuse had been slowed by moisture but the mechanism was still functioning. The charge exploded just as he threw himself backward and rolled downhill.

From the beginning each program was executed with full community participation. The young men lived with the villagers, gained their trust, learned their needs, and together planned the projects. The villagers were required to finance the schemes to the extent they were able—providing labor, local materials, some money, and by housing and feeding the volunteers. Soedjarwo agreed to find outside funding agencies to provide the balance. Through the efforts of Casutt the Ngembesan project was assisted by Australia's Community Aid Abroad (CAA), and the large Cankringan program by Australia's Freedom from Hunger Foundation and World University Services.

Adrian Harris, the director in Indonesia of the CAA, was impressed by the work of these young men and in 1972 pointed out to Soedjarwo that he could be funded directly, rather than through Father Casutt, if he formalized his organization. A name was the first requirement, so on the spur of the moment the group became Yayasan Dian Desa (Light of the Village Foundation). It was registered with capital holdings of Rp.5,000 (about US$12). Harris helped Dian Desa open a bank account to receive donations and then taught Soedjarwo how to write grant proposals.

The next year Robert Shaw of the Ford Foundation, who understood the difficulties of embryonic organizations and had faith in Soedjarwo's abilities, organized a meeting of foreign funding agencies in Jakarta and invited Soedjarwo to explain his work. The youth was greeted with some skepticism because of his relative lack of experience and his inability to guarantee success. But as Soedjarwo pointed out to his interrogators, if he could guarantee success he would go to a bank: "the reason I am coming to you is because I want you to share the risk." The Ford Foundation and OXFAM agreed to provide US$10,000 and US$14,000 respectively. These funds enabled Dian Desa to transform itself from a group of field workers into a formal nongovernmental organization (NGO). Soedjarwo asked Peter Hagul, whom he knew from student days, to become administrative director and together they found office space, purchased a filing cabinet, and set up a simple management system.

Dian Desa grew quickly and it soon became necessary to divide its activities into six sectors: Water, Agriculture, Food Technology, Energy, Small Industries and Social Sciences. Overall planning and policymaking was entrusted to a Secretariat, made up of the acting heads of the various sections, with Soedjarwo as Director. A non-voting Advisory Board was also formed to include outsiders in fields related to the foundation's work. With the establishment of this stable structure, Soedjarwo was finally able to take time off in 1974 to complete his degree in civil engineering.

In some respects the social sciences division of Dian Desa, although established last, is the most important; it is responsible for providing background material on the regions in which the foundation works. Since Dian Desa relies heavily on community participation, it is vital for its field workers to understand the social, religious, political and economic relationships within each village or group of villages. The social sciences sector also monitors projects to determine their success or lack of it. It works closely with technical experts, analyzing people's attitudes and fine-tuning projects as they progress. It also prepares feasibility studies for other community development organizations.

Eventually library and publications units were added to back up the social sciences section and to disseminate a record of the experiences of the other sectors. The library has an extensive collection of appropriate technology and development material and is an important source of data and ideas for Dian Desa, other NGOs, and government institutions. The publications section produces "how to" leaflets and a magazine to help disseminate new ideas and information to a broad range of readers.

The water section, the first unit of Dian Desa, by 1977 had developed an improved version of the hydraulic ram. The ram, which can lift water many times the height of its inflow pipes, requires no fuel—an obvious economic advantage, operating instead by the build-up of pressure from water flowing into a chamber. Moreover the pump has no moving parts other than the intake and outflow valves and is therefore easy to maintain. Within five years Dian Desa helped villagers install 12 such hydraulic systems. As with all foundation projects, the villagers financed part of the cost of building and installing the pumps. Maintenance funds were set up with each user-family contributing monthly. Dian Desa checks the books regularly to ensure the accounts are honest and to help the villagers master basic bookkeeping skills.

In unusually arid areas, where no springs were found and where village ponds dried up during the dry season, the foundation began (1978) to help villagers build water catchment tanks—4, 5, 9, 16 or 25 cubic meters in size, depending upon the number of families to be served. These concrete tanks, or cisterns, are reinforced with a framework of bamboo, or occasionally steel mesh. If properly managed they hold enough clean water to last throughout the dry season.

In the beginning, however, the villagers did not use the tanks correctly. Because they were conveniently located, they were used during the rainy season for normal household needs, with the result that little water remained for the dry months. Moreover, some villagers found the taste of rainwater too bland, and deliberately mixed pond mud with tank water to improve its flavor! Dian Desa instituted informal training programs and now 80 percent of the cisterns are properly used.

In 1980 the Indonesian government—which eight years earlier had recognized the work of the young student volunteers with an Economic Council Award—called on Dian Desa to build 5,000 water tanks as part of the government's Project for Village Development, a program funded in part by the World Bank. Within three years the foundation had trained 400 village-paid cadres who were capable of building 1,000 tanks a month and of teaching the villagers how to use them. (Dian Desa limited itself to training; it refused to procure the materials in order to protect itself from possible charges of graft or corruption.)

There was one major problem with regard to the water program which still remains. Whereas Dian Desa insists projects be funded as much as possible by the villagers themselves, politicians seeking votes are all too ready to build tanks in a village just before an election. The result, Soedjarwo says, is that politicians "destroy the spirit of the people" for their own political gain.

As early as 1978 UNICEF donated funds to the foundation for testing water supply innovations. Besides evaluating water tanks and hydralic pumps, Dian Desa tested purification systems and experimented with iodine to kill bacteria, and with the cooked seeds of the *Moringa oleifera* (a plant native to Java) to accelerate the sedimentation of impurities. Field workers now teach village women how to dry, grind and use the *Moringa* seeds. They also consult women on where to locate wells and train them in maintaining pumps. These responsibilities have given the women a greater sense of self worth and at the same time have enhanced their status within both the family and the community.

Agricultural projects have long been a concern of Soedjarwo and his colleagues. When they returned to villages where they had first developed water projects, they were disappointed to find the people were not making productive use of the time they saved in not having to travel long distances for water. Those saved hours, Soedjarwo reasoned, should be employed in income-generating activities.

He now laughs about their inexperience and early failures in selecting viable money crops. For example, the young engineers first persuaded the villagers to grow apples—in the tropical lowlands! The trees developed but produced no fruit. Oranges were another failure because of a virus that attacked the trees and permanently destroyed their fruiting ability. Later plantings of pineapple, coffee, cloves and winged beans have succeeded, and recently garlic and ginger have been planted in two areas of Java with excellent results. For these ventures Dian Desa now takes all the financial risks, the farmers supply the land and manpower, and profits are shared equally. Dian Desa encourages the farmers to set aside part of their profits to buy their own seed and fertilizer, thus permitting the foundation to diminish its financial input and free its funds for similar programs in new areas.

In the beginning marketing was a problem, not because markets did not exist, but because the village people lacked the simple management skills to take advantage of them. To avoid their being cheated by loan sharks and middlemen Soedjarwo himself served as the contact between the farmers and the markets or factories that purchased their crops. In the case of cloves, he went directly to the major cigarette factories—which use most of the cloves grown in the islands. In the case of coffee he helped the growers set up their own processing plant.

With a partial loan from OXFAM, Dian Desa in 1973 began a project to help villagers raise chickens, commercially, for eggs. The peasants quickly invested in the project but soon found they were at the mercy of big producers who manipulated the prices of fresh eggs. To overcome this disadvantage Dian Desa's food technologists developed a means of preserving eggs for up to six months, eliminating the need to sell the eggs immediately. The eggs are collected when they are no more than two days old—before bacteria have penetrated the shell. They are then sterilized with alcohol, dipped in a protective sealer of liquid paraffin, and kept on racks in a communal storage place until prices rise, usually just before major religious holidays.

In addition Dian Desa assists farmers in acquiring high quality seed; it has introduced more productive farming methods, simple new tools and machines, and it gives guidance according to individual need. It has also helped farmers form "pre-cooperative" credit unions, encouraging small groups of families participating in a common project to set aside funds for mutual borrowing and helping them establish a reasonable repayment schedule. Most of these small credit unions are working fairly well. Occasionally one will fail because a village strong man refuses to repay a loan, or because a large number of borrowers have used the funds for consumption rather than for business investment. But Dian Desa personnel, who have worked in the villages for many months, know who among the villagers are good credit risks and encourages limitation of membership to this element.

A recent program innovation is the Coastal Development Project to help villagers increase their incomes by "farming" brackish coastal ponds. The project is currently experimenting in shrimp farming. As in other programs Dian Desa assumes the initial capital risk; farmers use their land and labor and reap the profits. When the program is self-sufficient the foundation will remove itself from the scene and let market forces take over.

Early on the energy section became interested in the problem of cooking fuel, since the common village fuel is wood and the hillsides of Indonesia were fast being deforested. The unit first tried to develop an inexpensive biogas digester, utilizing human, animal and plant waste. Although it got the cost down to US$70, this was still too expensive for the average farmer.

The following year it turned its attention to promoting the use of a more efficient wood burning stove. The basic model chosen was designed in 1960 by Singer, of the Central Forestry Association of Switzerland. Modified in Guatemala, it was known as the Lorena Stove and was 50 to 60 percent more fuel-efficient than the traditional village unit.

In the beginning eight men were trained to make the Lorena stove and then sent back to their respective villages, charged with convincing their peers of its usefulness and with showing them how to construct it. Despite the efforts of these pioneers, a year later only 100 stoves had been built, and surveys showed that most were not being used.

One problem was the design. The original model was large, high and proved to be dangerous since in Indonesia children are frequently responsible for cooking meals. The design was therefore modified. Also the original stove had a flue to eliminate smoke, but many Indonesian households were accustomed to utilizing smoke to preserve grain stored in the rafters. Flues are now optional. Other design changes accommodated the need for cooking certain foods slowly and for preventing the ceramic materials, used in the manufacture of the stoves, from cracking.

The government expressed an interest in the Lorena stove and Dian Desa contracted to train personnel in the Department of Rural Development to build these new models. Seven thousand stoves were produced but their fuel efficiency proved to be less than that of traditional stoves. The government workers, in their haste to meet targets, had not paid attention to quality.

The foundation finally recognized it was unrealistic to expect individual farmers or inexperienced government workers to become stovemakers. It therefore turned to village potters—who were experienced in ceramics and whose industry had been declining since the advent of plastic—and convinced them to make the stoves for sale. These potter-made stoves, 30,000 of which have now been distributed, have a fuel efficiency of 18 percent, compared to 7 percent for traditional stoves, an improvement of over 150 percent. When properly installed, and with a mud covering added by the owner himself, the efficiency can be raised as high as 24 percent. Thus with these stoves Dian Desa has been responsible for improving the efficiency of the wood stove, of reducing the demand on the environment for firewood, and of establishing a new product for a declining craft. It hopes to make the use of the Lorena stove a national priority and to encourage its adoption in other developing countries.

In 1978 Dian Desa recognized that the foundation itself needed to become at least partially self-supporting. "Every day we talked to the villagers about self-reliance," says Soedjarwo, "but in the foundation we were completely dependent on funds from the outside." Dian Desa, therefore, came up with three income-generating projects: a workshop, a winged bean factory and consultancy services.

The workshop was begun immediately. About half its workload was devoted to research and the development of appropriate technology for the foundation's own programs. Outside workshops, Soedjarwo had found, were generally unwilling to spend their time on experimental products, and if willing, usually charged an exorbitant price. The other half was scheduled for government and commercial needs. For example, the workshop manufactured mechanical driers, grinders and centrifugal separators, the latter sophisticated machines that previously were imported from Germany at a cost of approximately US$85,000 each. Since he had lower labor and overhead costs, and no import duties, Soedjarwo was able to sell a separator for US$5,000.

Dian Desa is presently working on a solar drier for drying pineapple, coffee, corn and cassova, and is experimenting with a solar-operated sterilizer for rural hospital use. It is also interested in developing a steam engine fueled by rice husks and other agricultural waste, and a biomass gasification unit to power an ordinary diesel engine and produce electricity for rural villages. All production from the workshop, commercial or otherwise, is limited to "appropriate technology," i.e. items which can be produced within a reasonable budget, maintained easily and have relevance for the developmental needs of the nation.

The second fund-raising project, the winged bean factory, was started in 1980 by the workshop, in conjunction with the small industries unit. In the course of experimentation it was found that neither of its first products, oil and flour—both of which are highly nutritious, could compete on the market with coconut oil and wheat flour. The factory therefore began producing bean catsup and bean meal for *tempe,* a fermented cake popular in Indonesian cuisine.

The consultancy service is really Soedjarwo. He is a sought-after advisor to foreign developmental organizations, such as USAID and the World Bank. He acknowledges: "as far as rural development in Indonesia is concerned, I am better qualified than an outsider with a Ph.D. who doesn't know either the language or the culture." He charges international consultancy fees and donates 65 percent of the fee to the foundation.

Dian Desa has been remarkably fortunate in attracting and keeping an outstanding staff despite the low wages it pays. Anton Lowa, the head of the water supply sector, was one of the group that started the initial field work with Soedjarwo in 1968. Didik Priyono and Slamet Sudarmadji, who have been with Dian Desa since 1974 and 1976 respectively, are responsible for many innovations in food technology. These men, along with Paulus Sugiono, who is in charge of the workshop, and Peter Hagul, now head of the social sciences division, keep Dian Desa running smoothly during Soedjarwo's frequent travels on field trips and consultancies. Two of Soedjarwo's brothers, Edwin and Aryanto, also work with the foundation, Edwin as chief administrator and head of publications, and Aryanto as head of the fuel-efficient stove section of the energy division.

Throughout the years Soedjarwo has maintained good relations with Gajah Mada University. In the late 1970s he taught at the institution and helped incorporate courses in appropriate technology into the curriculum. The rector invited Dian Desa to become an institute of the university but Soedjarwo declined, preferring to retain the flexibility of an independent organization. Nonetheless Dian Desa takes 50–70 Gajah Mada students a years (for 2–3 months) as field workers. One of its objectives "is to open the eyes of the students to the reality of the daily lives of the majority of Indonesians."

The foundation also coorperates with university and government personnel in developing projects on islands other than Java. In the late 1970s Soedjarwo assisted his former professor, Hardjoso, in designing a project to reclaim swampland on the island of Kalimantan (Borneo) as part of the government's resettlement program. He devised a canal and gate system to reclaim the swamp, using the tides as an energy source. In 1979 the foundation opened a branch office on the island of Timor, having been invited by the government to assist in planning and developing the Nusatenggara Timur Province Area Development Program, a project funded jointly by the Indonesian government and USAID. In all, Dian Desa has or has had programs on Java (Yogyakarta, Central Java and East Java), Kalimantan, Madura, Timor and South Sulawesi.

Rather than open more branch offices, however, the foundation has decided to train personnel from other nongovernmental organizations (NGOs) to work along Dian Desa lines. The first session of the Rural Water Supply Training Program was opened in Yogyakarta in 1983 with 28 participants—from Java, Flores, Irian, North Sumatra and Timor. The program was co-financed by participating organizations and Canada's International Development Research Centre. Training in technical aspects of supplying water to rural areas was supplemented by instruction in motivation and communication skills. A similar program was started in the field of small industries.

The foundation has built up an extensive information service on appropriate technology. It cooperates in this field with international organizations such as Volunteer in International Technical Assistance, Intermediate Technology Development Group of Great Britain, and World University Services, and has accepted members of Stanford University's Volunteers in Asia for one-year study-work programs.

Dian Desa maintains good relations with all levels of government. Anxious to avoid jealousy, it takes little credit for its work, acknowledging instead the input of the various governmental levels and of the people. Local officials are honored guests at opening ceremonies of all completed projects. Special rapport with the Ministry of Environment has existed since Minister Emil Salim agreed in 1978 to serve on Dian Desa's advisory board. It was Salim who proposed Soedjarwo for the Presidential Award for Environmental Development which Soedjarwo received in 1980.

Before Salim's interest, non-profit NGOs did not have particularly high standing with the government. The government tended to equate the term "non-profit" with "charity," and assumed such bodies were automatically pressure groups. In the last ten years, however, by working with NGOs such as Dian Desa, the government has come to appreciate the advantages of sharing the burden of development with the non-profit sector. NGOs need no continuing government subsidy; they often have extensive operating experience, and they have their own networks for reaching target groups. A project undertaken in conjunction with an NGO usually costs much less than a project undertaken by the government alone.

Soedjarwo believes that NGOs are also an indication of, and an impetus for, democratization. Their most important contribution, he says, is their ability to involve people in their own development; they have the time and flexibility to do so. Moreover NGOs, unlike government bureaucracies, are not mandated to fulfill targets within a specified period, nor given a project to implement that may not seem meaningful to the people "being helped." On the contrary, NGOs can take time to determine the needs perceived by the people themselves and enlist their interest and their support. (For example, Soedjarwo lived four months in the village of Morotai in 1972 before he talked to the villagers about the water project he had in mind. He gave the people—who had previously been promised much by the government that was never delivered—time to learn to know and trust him.) An emotional, rather than a rational, relationship needs to develop, Soedjarwo believes, and NGOs have the time to create such rapport.

Soedjarwo is also convinced that transmitters of a new technology must reach out to the lower economic classes and convince them that the new techniques are beneficial to *them,* not just to the village leadership. Agents of transmission must be flexible and must be able to build upon the existing technology of the village; encourage habits that will maximize the benefits derived from the new technology; and evolve means to disseminate the new technology and promote its use. To be successful, Soedjarwo emphasizes, transmitters must convince people the ideas for change are theirs, give them credit for their input, and make them responsible for the outcome. At every step the contributions and emotional support of the villagers are essential.

Soedjarwo frequently travels abroad, both to study and advise. His first foreign experience was attending a three-month course in rural development at the Asian Institute of Technology in Thailand in 1976, followed by attendance in 1978 at the Center for Appropriate Technology, Technical School, in Delft, Holland. More recently his travels have taken him to Latin America, Africa and China under the auspices of the United Nations University and World University Services—on whose Executive Committee he served from 1976 to 1980. Although he travels as much as seven months a year, when he is in Indonesia he lives modestly with his wife, Kartika Kumala Sutrisnohadi, whom he married in 1975. Kartika herself has worked with Dian Desa, serving as treasurer for four years.

Government and private institutions, both Indonesian and foreign, have in recent years recognized Anton Soedjarwo's dedication and expertise. In 1983 the Magsaysay Award Foundation gave him its Award for Community Leadership for "stimulating Javanese villagers to genuine self-reliance with simple, readily applicable appropriate technology." His greatest tribute, however, came back in 1976 when his son was born by Caesarean section. Soedjarwo was informed at 4 a.m. that his wife would need a blood transfusion; by 7 a.m. six truckloads of villagers had arrived to offer blood. His rapport with the people has never wavered.

Rehabilitation to Self Help

Fazle Hasan Abed

Bangladesh is both blessed and cursed by the mighty Padma, formed as the Ganges and Brahmaputra rivers join to carry the immense rainfall of the Himalayas to the Bay of Bengal. During the rainy season floods, exacerbated by cyclones (typhoons), inundate much of the land, land which in turn lies parched during the dry season. But the alluvial soil of this vast delta complex is inherently fertile. Early in this century the region, then known as East Bengal and part of the British Indian Empire, was a surplus food producing area and known affectionately by its people as *Shonar Bangla*—Golden Bengal. In recent times the area has been saddled with rapid population growth and beset by political problems and frequent ecologial disasters.

When the subcontinent was divided in 1947 between India and Pakistan, East Bengal became East Pakistan, separated by 1,600 kilometers from West Pakistan, separated by 1,600 kilometers from West Pakistan. The relationship between East and West Pakistan was always uneasy and in 1971 it deteriorated into a war for the "liberation" of East Pakistan. At the cost of tens of thousands dead and wounded, millions of refugees and tremendous physical destruction, the state of Bangladesh (country of the Bengalis) was established on December 16, 1971.

The new nation lacked transportation facilities, public health programs and trained government personnel. But the problem that Fazle Hasan Abed addressed in 1972 was the fundamental one of food and shelter for the some 10 million refugees returning from haven in India to their shattered homeland.

The sixth of eight children of Siddiq and Sufia Khatun Hasan, Muslim landowners, Fazle Hasan was born April 27, 1936 in Sylhet, Bengal. Although named Fazle, the boy was always called Abed by his family, and when he grew up he took Abed as his second surname, the name by which he is universally known.

Abed received a traditional education through high school, but his university and post graduate careers were eclectic. He studied general science for two years, followed by a few months of physics at Dhaka University, before he elected to pursue a career in naval architecture at the University of Glasgow, Scotland. Graduating and practicing his profession for a brief time, he again changed direction and registered for a five-year professional course at the Chartered Institute of Cost and Management Accountants in London. At the same time he worked in financial and accounting departments in several industrial and commercial firms to gain practical experience and to meet institute requirements, a good preparation for one who would be handling hundreds of thousands of dollars in relief funds and grants.

Abed completed his course and in 1964 was elected an Associate Member of the Chartered Institute of Cost and Management Accountants. Four years later, to hone further his already impressive skills, he took a one-year computer science course at Toronto University in Canada.

Thus extremely well trained, Abed returned to Pakistan in 1969 to become Treasurer, and then Finance Director and Member of the Board, of Pakistan Shell Oil Company, a company based in Chittagong, East Pakistan's main port. His future as a member of his country's economic elite seemed assured.

What changed Abed's life for all time was the devastating cyclone which struck East Pakistan in 1970. It left in its wake 200,000 dead and countless thousands homeless and starving. Abed immediately plunged into relief work, enlisting his friends to start an organization called Heartland Emergency Lifesaving Project (HELP), which successfully gave immediate reconstructive aid to the cyclone victims.

While he was still involved with HELP the political tension that had been building up between East and West Pakistan exploded. In March 1971 the political leaders of East Pakistan were arrested and martial law was imposed. The Bengali resistance to this action led to civil war, with India supporting the now proclaimed independent state of Bangladesh.

Feeling he could best assist his country by soliticing support and funds among his many friends and contacts abroad, Abed resigned from Shell Oil and flew to London. There he formed "Action Bangladesh" to support the liberation struggle, and "Help Bangladesh" to garner funds for the freedom fighters and the some 10,000,000 refugees who were streaming across the border into India. During the next eight months Abed commuted between London and the Indian city of Calcutta—from which the relief supplies he obtained were channeled to the refugees and to the war front. In December 1971 Bangladesh gained its independence and Abed returned to his homeland.

The material damage caused by the war was estimated by the United Nations at US$1,200 million, with the loss of agricultural output at US$300 million and damage to housing—which consisted mainly of bamboo huts—at US$200 million. Food was scarce, and many of the work animals and fishing boats had been destroyed. With a population of around 75 million, Bangladesh had a population density of approximately 500 per square kilometer; its annual per capital income was estimated at US$70.

Abed realized that merely repairing previously existing facilities would be painfully insufficient for the needs of the new nation; a more complete scheme for rural development was necessary. But in the beginning he concentrated on helping people pull their shattered lives together. He took the money left from Help Bangladesh and founded the Bangladesh Rehabilitation Assistance Committee (BRAC), renamed the Bangladesh Rural Advancement Committee when the philosophic orientation of the organization broadened.

Abed focused his immediate rehabilitation efforts in the Sulla, Derai and Baniyachong *thanas* (subdistricts) of his home province of Sylhet, a region of 415 square kilometers with a population of 120,000. It was one of areas most devastated, least physically accessible, and least likely, Abed felt, to receive major relief support from other volunteer agencies.

Combining vision with common sense and exceptional management skills, the erstwhile accountant first organized a group of volunteers to survey the area in order to find out how many houses, head of cattle and boats had been destroyed, and how many families needed seed and fertilizer. His goal at this point was to return the villagers to their normal agricultural practices. When the survey was completed Abed recruited 45 "idealistic, unemployed Dhaka University graduates," at volunteer salaries, to help him process the data. On the basis of the results he formulated a project whose initial aims were to provide housing units for 8,000 (later 10,200) families, seeds and fertilizer for farmers, and boats and fishing nets for fishermen. He took his project propoasl to OXFAM (U.K. and Canada) which immediately granted him the US$400,000 necessary to implement it.

Dividing his recruits into groups Abed deployed them in the project area. There they set about separating people into four categories according to need. People who owned three acres (1.2 hectares) or more of land were charged 500 *taka* (US$91) for housing materials; those with between .4 and 1.2 hectares were charged Tk.200; and those with less than .4 hectare Tk.100. About half the people were landless in that, although they possessed their own house-lots, they were farmers who owned no cultivable land or fishermen who did not own their own boats. These landless were charged nothing.

Regardless of the fee charged, each family was eventually provided with Tk.500 worth of bamboo and galvanized iron sheets to build a new home. Meanwhile the government offered emergency food relief and UNICEF provided a milk supplement for the children. In addition each family received seeds for a vegetable garden.

Assembling the building materials taxed Abed's talents. Bamboo and timber had to be cut in the hills of India (Bangladesh as a flood plain has little wood) and floated by BRAC recruits down the river—some 15 to 20 days—in rafts stretching up to two miles in length. The galvanized iron sheets for roofing had to be imported from Japan and were delayed because the ports were clogged with relief cargo. Abed finally borrowed 1,000 tons of sheeting from the government, barged it to Sulla and began the rebuilding program, replacing the sheeting when his stock cleared customs. Three hundred boats were built and turned over to the fishermen without cost so they could resume their livelihood and protein would again be available.

The relief phase of the Sulla Project lasted from March to December 1972 and supplied the villagers with the bare essentials they needed for survival: houses, boats, fishing nets. Abed now turned his attention to the wider problem of establishing rural institutions and infrastructure, with the ultimate goal of developing the capabilities of the people so that they could take over the programs initiated by BRAC. His proposal to develop community centers, educational programs and primary health care delivery systems was funded (US$506,000) by OXFAM. He hired 35 additional university graduates to help implement the project, bringing the total to 80. Top students, these young people were still imbued with post-independence idealism.

BRAC also hired four doctors—like the students idealistic in the aftermath of the struggle for independence—to prepare an 11-month training course for paramedics who were to be instructed in primary health care. The paramedics were to be drawn from among the villagers. The first ones to be selected had a modicum of education, but it was soon discovered that persons with even a small amount of formal education were more interested in finding better jobs elsewhere than in serving their communities. And those who stayed tended to assume an elitist attitude, psychologically separating themselves from the poorer classes.

BRAC therefore changed its selection process and chose trainees from among newly organized groups of the village poor. These—usually illiterates—were given six months of training. They spent one day a week in the classroom where they studied basic public health, sanitation and simple curative procedures, and the other six days in the village where they practiced what they had learned. To prevent the paramedic trainees from developing into a professional class, their tasks were considered part of a joint group activity and they were either not reimbursed or their payment was turned over to the group.

In the end, the paramedics were taught not only how to

prevent disease, but how to treat the 15 major diseases—mainly intestinal and respiratory—which cause about 98 percent of all village illnesses; medicines were color-coded to facilitate identification. When villagers had ailments clearly beyond the scope of the paramedics, they were immediately referred to medical stations.

Although the villagers were at first wary of these new practitioners and their lack of formal education, they soon discovered they could explain their problems to them more easily than to the educated professionals. For the first several years the trainees were all male: BRAC could not find a woman doctor willing to spend time in the field training female paramedics until 1977.

During this second and expanded phase of the Sulla Project Abed and his colleagues began tackling the major problem of education. Their original plan envisioned eliminating illiteracy in Sulla within three years by conducting two courses a year at "literacy centers." Although 255 literacy centers were opened, a high dropout rate, diminishing community interest and recurring flood damage resulted in the closure of more than half the centers and discontinuation of many others. At the same time Abed recognized the shortcomings of a purely academic literacy program—i.e. using materials not relevant to the situations encountered by the average villager—and sought to recast BRAC's program in terms of "functional education."

He turned for assistance to World Education of New York, which helped BRAC hire consultants familiar with the ideas of Paolo Freire, a great Brazilian educationist whose books Abed had read and whose experiences in Brazil coincided with Abed's in Bangladesh.

Abed realized he had to learn from the villagers themselves, what they conceived their problems to be and how they wished to solve them. Functional education would give them a way to discuss their problems, and by assuming responsibility for their own actions they would not only move to ameliorate their conditions, but regain a sense of dignity and self respect. What Abed sought from World Education, therefore, was to learn techniques for eliciting village responses; on the basis of these responses BRAC could develop teaching materials according to Bangladeshi needs.

In May 1974 BRAC set up (with the aid of a US$92,000 grant from OXFAM) a Materials Development Unit consisting of three writers, one illustrator and one advisor. The first consultant for the project was Leon Clark from the Center for International Education at the University of Massachusetts.

Clark arrived during yet another disastrous flood. The water inside BRAC headquarters was "just below mattress level in the living quarters," and "filled with fish, snakes and frogs." Yet at any one time there were half a dozen people, perched on bedsteads or windowsills, discussing the project and making recommendations.

Despite Abed's intentions, and this initial staff enthusiasm, Clark found it difficult to convince the educational research staff that it could—and must—learn from the villagers their needs and goals. As Abed noted: "elitism is very much engrained in our culture . . . the whole concept of learning from the people was alien."

The university recruits were convinced they knew the problems; why ask the poor what they were? The development of educational materials necessitated, then, an investigation into the whole behavioral system of Bangladeshi society which, as it got underway, completely transformed BRAC's way of looking at rural development. In essence BRAC itself had to become a learning organization, with a flexible, adaptive approach.

As an early exercise Clark asked the unit workshop to list the needs which the villagers themselves had cited. "At first," he wrote, "many unfelt needs, urban or Western projections, were listed. But going back to the sources, we found time and time again that villagers had not in fact expressed those needs. In the end the list of felt needs was very short indeed, consisting only of four items: land ownership, housing, low-priced commodities and food. With these needs in mind, we began selecting topics for the individual lessons."[1]

Although the researchers seemed to agree with the findings and accept the new teaching methods and the evolving materials, Clark soon realized that they remained basically unconvinced,

---

1. Leon Clark. "A Consultant's Journal: Bangladesh," *Reports*. Dacca: BRAC. No. 13, November 1976.)

still believing that teachers should *teach,* and that classes should focus on *literacy* rather than *content.*

Feeling strongly that he, as an outsider, should not try to impose his views on the group drawing up the teaching materials, Clark turned to Abed. The latter's ability to work with and persuade people without arousing opposition or hostility enabled him to discuss with unit personnel the advantages of trying the new method. He finally convinced them when he suggested they test the new literacy approach on non-readers in the BRAC office before using it in a village setting.

The Materials Unit eventually developed 60 core lessons, all of which have been tested and revised four times, most recently in 1986. These lessons were designed to deal with the major issues affecting the lives of the rural population and to provide the villagers with the necessary level of literacy and mathematical skill to address them. Each lesson dealt with a problem which the villagers discussed in light of their own understanding; the problem was not explained to them. Materials included 139 charts, a lesson book containing the 60 lessons and a teacher's manual. The average class lasted four months and consisted of 20–40 adults. Games were used to reinforce the lessons, games to which the villagers were accustomed.

Blind Man's Bluff, for instance, was used with women to increase group participation and instill a sense of shared common feelings. After the women had enjoyed playing the BRAC worker would suggest the game expressed something about life:

"What do you feel when you are blindfolded," she would ask.

"Darkness!"

"Have you ever felt in the dark: helpless, dependent?"

"When we were first married!"

"When we had our first child!"

As these responses were elicited the women began to realize they shared many of the same doubts and worries, and a sense of community emerged.

Abed found the rural people responded well to this new approach, although the university recruits who taught it often had the same elitist attitude that had made the research and development staff skeptical. When the success of the program was established, however, other social welfare organizations requested use of the new materials; Abed was delighted to accommodate them. However when the government invited BRAC to supply materials for its national education program, Abed refused. He felt the government's priority of literacy, rather than of raising the awareness of people to development possibilities, was in error. If BRAC participated in the government effort and it failed, he feared BRAC's materials, rather than the government's approach, would be blamed.

BRAC still recruits its staff among university graduates. From a total of 400 applicants, the organization weeds out, by a series of examinations and interviews, all but 10—and of those perhaps 5 will stay. During the interviews each applicant is scrutinized for his/her communication ability, attitude toward rural development, likelihood of leaving to take work elsewhere, and "whether the economic pressure in his family is just right." BRAC finds that generalists, and the "poor, but not too poor," are most suitable.

After graduates are recruited they are given a short orientation course and are then apprenticed to senior workers in the field. Three months later they return to the training center where they find their courses more meaningful, seen in the light of actual experience. Some of the original recruits have become directors of other voluntary agencies, and BRAC's philosophy and influence in education and training programs has thereby spread. BRAC also sells or makes its materials available to other NGOs.

In the late 1970s BRAC expanded its development work into Manikganj, an agricultural area of 198 square kilometers near Dhaka, with a population density of 840 per square kilometer. Sixty percent of the population was Muslim and 40 percent Hindu. BRAC's approach in Manikganj was to promote its rural development activities through local youth organizations, women's groups and cooperative societies, using a minimum of BRAC personnel. Abed began the project, which was funded by Brot fur der Welt (Bread for the World) of Germany, by promoting developmental awareness through functional education programs. In order to create the dialogue necessary for a sense of group identity and cohesion to emerge, it was necessary to identify homogeneous groups: i.e., the landed and the landless obviously did not share the same concerns.

To separate the landed from the landless BRAC began food-for-work programs, reasoning correctly that only the latter would participate. The programs were designed, however, to fulfill the needs identified as priorities by the village as a whole—the construction of roads, canals and irrigation channels.

The strategy in Manikganj, then, as in Sulla, was to identify the poorest group, and through functional education, give its members the psychological capability of changing their lives. The strategy was based on two premises: first, that people, even the poorest, want to make their own decisions and support themselves rather than accept handouts from others; and second, that poverty actually arises from powerlessness. BRAC's goal, therefore, was to reduce the powerlessness of the poor by showing them how to organize themselves and act together.

For the poor to realize they can change the social order, he reasoned, they must first understand their problems are caused, not by God or fate, but by the structure of society. Accordingly, in workshop discussions BRAC induced the landless villagers to talk about the society in which they found themselves, the kinds of exploitation they were subjected to and their causes. BRAC then sought to help the villagers create systems to reduce that exploitation.

Problems dealt with in Manikganj by the newly organized landless included, for example, the food-for-work program itself. They discussed the quantity and quality of the food, how to check corruption in its handling and distribution, and the value of the work undertaken.

Women were often particularly responsive, especially when they realized that social customs which they had assumed to be immutable—e.g. easy divorces for men and heavy expenditures for family festivities—were in fact changeable.

Since a major problem faced by the poor everywhere is the loss of land to moneylenders, who are at the same time often the major landowners. BRAC sought to help the workshops devise alternative financial sources such as cooperative credit unions.

Another problem is the insufficient wage paid manual labor.

BRAC helped the laborers in Manikganj understand that to acquire some control over wages they had to organize themselves at harvest time when labor was short. The first time the landless tried to organize the landlords attempted to import workers from other areas. Although the laborers blocked the "scab" labor, they realized that in order to succeed in their effort they would have to organize the surrounding villages to prevent strike-breaking. Thus of their own accord the laborers went to neighboring villages to organize their leaders. Now, says Abed, "if you have 200 villages and organize 15, you've effectively organized the area."

Action did not stop with organization, however. BRAC found that false criminal charges were being brought against the landless leaders by powerful landlords and began providing legal services for the accused. It now tries to persuade the groups themselves to put aside funds for legal aid from their own savings.

Ironically, there are dangers inherent in the system of self-help, Abed notes, and it is important to find the kind of programs which will create solidarity in a group, not divisiveness. For example, if an area of 200 families can support 40 cows, you cannot establish a program that permits 40 families to obtain a cow each without creating a split between them and the other 160 family units.

The sense of cooperation achieved in group workshops is also very fragile and can disintegrate quickly if it has not reached a level where the people feel a strong vested interest in keeping the cooperative spirit going. This fragility, in turn, makes it difficult for BRAC workers to extricate themselves from a program and turn it over to the people concerned.

Nevertheless by the early 1980s Abed felt the Sulla Project had reached the point of self-sufficiency and self-direction. "When we find landless groups adjudicating in various village conflicts," he says, "we feel they're becoming powerful. When women organize themselves to fight against divorces or multiple marriages, or when village laborers fight to divert a road . . . that would, if built, take employment away from them, they are using their power."[2] Other examples of the power of the landless

---

2. Abed, taped interview, in Ramon Magsaysay Award Foundation files.

groups are when they identify programs the government *should* undertake, rather than accept those the government proposes, and when they demand services (such as medical care) which a government agency is *supposed* to provide but has not.

Over the years Abed recognized that a village organization not only has to have leaders who are trusted by and responsive to the group, but it has to have *joint leadership* so that one person cannot assume all power unto himself. Joint leadership comes about when expertise is divided, e.g. when one person becomes knowledgeable in health education, a second in power pump mechanics and a third in functional education.

In cooperatives, moreover, BRAC insists on *joint responsibility* in all aspects of policy, management and expenditure. Corruption and mismanagement, such as private use of the society's savings, misallocation of inputs and the extension of credit, have traditionally beset cooperatives. Therefore BRAC insists that all decisions concerning the acquisition and spending of funds must be taken jointly. Some money may be spent individually, but only to the extent that group interest and solidarity are not reduced. Such a rule is ultimately advantageous to the individual. If, for example, the cooperative helps a woman buy a cow as part of a joint program and the cow dies, the group, not the woman alone, absorbs the financial loss.

Aside from helping organize cooperatives geared to the interests of the poor, BRAC has been involved in providing credit for specific projects. Here, too, it fosters self-reliance. It does not give credit "too fast or too easily," but waits until the group has successfully undertaken some joint activities with its own resources. When it has proven itself BRAC may provide partial credit. Credit is advanced at 12 percent interest, far better than the often 200–300 percent charged by moneylenders. BRAC has found the repayment rate to be fairly good except in years when flooding has ruined village crops. At such times the loan has to be rescheduled over three or four years and the interest is often written off.

In 1978 BRAC decided a bank was needed to serve the landless who could not offer security for loans. The bank would provide group loans for group projects. At precisely that time, however, the government nationalized banks and declined to give BRAC a permit to open a new one. Instead it gave BRAC permission to operate a Rural Credit and Training Program (RCTP). Accordingly, branches were set up in eight *thanas* throughout Bangladesh to provide training, logistical support, and money for the landless. The project was funded by NOVIB (Netherlands Organization for International Assistance). NOVIB money was used also as a revolving fund for loans. By 1984 there were 20 branch offices working with 451 male and 376 female groups in 390 villages. The total credit disbursed was Tk35,545,790, with an on-time repayment rate of 80 percent. As their capability increases, along with their capital requirements, the groups should outgrow their dependency upon BRAC and receive credit directly from government agricultural and industrial banks.

Research and evaluation are another important aspect of BRAC's operations. Researchers are drawn, not only from the field staff, but from the villagers themselves. For example, the villagers are asked to determine how the village power structure, which handles the distribution of resources, actually works. The field workers—rather than the office staff—collate this information, thus not only gaining firsthand information of the problems to be dealt with, but respect for the villagers' insight and acumen.

Currently BRAC administers 17 different projects and activities. The Manikganj Project alone includes 301 village organizations in 182 villages and 15 union coordinating committees. A project in Jamalpur is specifically geared to increasing the ability of women to think creatively and improve the economic and physical health of their families. The Training and Resource Center in Savar, and the nearby Center for Rural Development Workers, train villagers and field workers in agriculture, poultry raising and fish farming.

A high priority in all BRAC project areas is family planning. With a population in 1988 of 100 million Bangladesh has a population density second only to the island state of Singapore, and the highest percent of land under cultivation in the world with the exception of the island state of Barbados. Unless its growth rate is drastically reduced it faces a doubling of the population in 25 years. BRAC has trained Lady Family Planning

Organizers (LFPO) who go from house to house in their own villages to motivate their clients to enroll in family planning clinics. They follow up on acceptors, and in the case of side effects or complications refer the acceptor to a paramedic or doctor as the case demands.

BRAC also runs the Oral Therapy Extension Program, a nationwide program seeking to reach one female in each household to teach her how to make and administer oral rehydration fluid (a salt, sugar, water solution), that is a specific for the diarrheal diseases which frequently cause the death of children. By 1987 the program had reached some 7 million families. BRAC also cooperates with the government in immunizing children against the five major child-killers (diptheria, whooping cough, polio, measles and tetanus), and women of child-bearing age against tetanus, a major cause of death in childbirth. It also assists in the national distribution of Vitamin A.

A multi-faceted development organization with a staff of over 2,500 men and women, BRAC has organized some 2,500 continuing self-reliant groups in some 1,500 villages. Its annual operating budget is approximately Tk.160 million (US$5.3 million). Practicing what it preaches to its project participants, BRAC has sought to assure its own financial self-reliance. Its first venture was a quality commercial printing press. The press began by handling the organization's functional education materials and journal, *Gonokendra* (Community Center), which is distributed free to some schools but sold to others. Today the press earns US$100,000 annually from commercial contracts; it occupies the ground floor of a BRAC built and owned five-story building in Dhaka.

BRAC's second commercial project, which serves the community, as well as earns project operating income, was Aarong (Village Fair); a marketing outlet for handicrafts. Aarong became self-sustaining within one year, and now has four shops in three cities employing some 80 persons. Domestic sales total approximately Tk.22,000,000 and export sales are developing. In 1984 a Cold Storage and Ice Plant was opened which can store 3,854 metric tons of potatoes a year and produce 10 tons of ice per day. BRAC also charges all the projects it administers about seven percent of the project's overhead costs, including staff salaries and headquarters expenses.

Abed lives in Dhaka. From there he can readily travel to various BRAC projects around the country. Moreover, living in the capital he can remain in close touch with the government, with international lending bodies and with other national voluntary agencies. Far from allowing competition or conflicts to arise between BRAC and the other volunteer groups, BRAC provides support for all who request it—primarily through training programs and materials.

Those who have worked closely with BRAC are often struck by how much the organization reflects Abed's own style—calm, quiet, humble yet forceful, rational and objective. Perhaps the most striking attribute Abed has conveyed to BRAC is his profound faith in the rural poor and in their ability to solve their own problems. The Magsaysay Award Foundation honored him for these qualities with an award in Community Leadership in 1980, commending him for "demonstrating that Bangladeshi solutions are valid for the needs of the rural poor in his burdened country."

Pragmatic Socialist

Zafrullah Chowdhury

The fear of illness and the often exorbitant cost of treatment and medicine is shared by hundreds of millions of people in the developing world. Families are frequently driven into permanent debt by the calamity illness brings and many invest their scant savings in medicines that are worthless and sometimes even harmful. Their predicament has been compounded by ignorance, and by lax professional and government monitoring of the pharmaceutical industry.

Zafrullah Chowdhury has spent his life seeking to improve the health of Bangladeshi villagers, treat their illnesses and provide them with safe, inexpensive medication. At the same time, he has been consciously trying to raise the educational and skill levels of the villagers, and the status of village women. Real progress in rural development can only be achieved, he believes, when the exploitation of one class by another ceases, and when women, the most exploited segment of society, achieve dignity and greater financial security.

Zafrullah as born December 27, 1941, in Quepara, a village outside Chittagong, in East Bengal, India (today Bangladesh). Just two years later the "great Bengal famine" claimed the lives of over one-million peasants. His land-owning family, rich by local standards, suffered little and did what it could by sharing its surplus with the hungry. His mother's stories of the starving pleading at their door for anything of nutritional value—even the water used to wash rice—impressed upon the boy at an early age the disparity between the rich and the poor, and the pain of those born into poverty.

Hasina Begum Chowdhury, his gentle mother, was a highly intelligent woman, but as she came from a strict Muslim family which did not believe in the education of women, had only five years of schooling. His father, H. M. Chowdhury, was an All-India hockey and football player; recruited by the police to play on their teams, he eventually joined the force, serving as a senior police officer in Calcutta until 1947. He transferred to Dhaka, the capital of the eastern province of the new state of Pakistan, when the sub-continent was partitioned.

The eldest of ten brothers and sisters, Zafrullah entered school in Dhaka and spent his primary and high school years there. He was a good student, and like his father, an accomplished athlete. Nevertheless his athletic interests were secondary to his pride in his scholastic achievements; the year a young uncle surpassed him in class-standing he abandoned sports completely. He blames this impetuous decision on his temperment. "I was an angry person," he recalls, and quickly adds, "I am still an angry person." But now it is social injustice that arouses him.

On merit scholarships throughout his school years, Chowdhury was readily accepted at Dhaka Medical College when he decided to take his mother's advice and become a doctor. He graduated in 1964 and completed one year of internship before he left for England where he continued his surgical training in various British hospitals, at the same time studying to become a Fellow of the Royal College of Surgeons (FRCS). In spite of the pressures of surgical training he found the time and money to indulge his taste for fine living, flying and fast cars.

The young surgeon-playboy did not achieve his advanced degree. Within a week of his final examination fighting broke out in East Pakistan between the army and Bengali dissidents, and he decided to forego both the FRCS for which he had worked so long, and his life of pleasure.

The decision was again in character. During his student days

Chowdhury had been politically active, organizing protests against social injustice, and agitating for educational reform and increased political power for East Bengal. When the country was under martial law in 1962 he had helped organize a doctors' strike. It was suppressed by the government and Chowdhury and other leaders were incarcerated for several days in the Dhaka Central Jail. Though not a card carrying member, he was ideologically commited to the left wing of the Awami (People's) League and espoused socialism.

In London Chowdhury had maintained his contact with doctors, university professors, union leaders and other Bengalis who were seeking to end martial law in Pakistan and to achieve economic parity for East Pakistan vis-a-vis West Pakistan. The elections of December 1970 brought into sharp focus the conflict between the two sectors of the bifurcated nation, and on March 27, 1971 the leader of the outgoing national regime undertook military action against East Pakistan. Army tanks attacked Dhaka University and street riots and civil war followed.

In England Chowdhury threw himself into the war effort, helping form a committee to raise money and sway British and world opinion in support of the newly declared state of Bangladesh. As battlefield casualties rapidly mounted, however, he became dissatisfied with his supportive role. There were few trained surgeons in Bangladesh to administer to the injured and, he reasoned, each untreated casualty could demoralize scores of healthy soldiers. He and fellow doctor Mohammad Abdul Mobin decided to leave for the front. As the heaviest fighting was along the eastern border between Bangladesh and India, the two offered their services to the commanders there. But the priority of the generals was arms, not bandages.

Discouraged but determined, the young doctors sold their automobiles and other possessions in England, and with the proceeds built a makeshift hospital on the Indian side of the border near the Bangladeshi town of Comilla. The hospital was a collection of tents and thatched huts. Tree branches tied together with ropes and covered with bamboo served as beds. Their limited supplies were generously augmented by donations of medicine and equipment from the British medical profession and other private British supporters.

Lack of trained assistants was an immediate problem. Since it takes years to train a nurse, the young doctors had to be innovative. Chowdhury had followed with interest China's experiment with "barefoot doctors"—illiterate villagers taught to treat common diseases and administer emergency aid to accident victims. The nearby refugee camps were teeming with young women eager to assist in the war effort, so the doctors decided to draw upon this pool and train "barefoot nurses and paramedics." Not only did the young women learn quickly, they proved to be tireless workers. After treating the soldiers they would attend to refugees and the rural poor. The hospital eventually expanded to 480 beds, with the outlying centers set up to treat refugees and local villagers.

The war ended abruptly in December 1971 following intervention by the Indian Army. Bangladesh had gained its independence, but the new nation was in disarray—its economy shattered, the Provisional Government disorganized, and many of the new officials as corrupt as those who had just been defeated. Chowdhury, unsure of government support, prepared to dismantle his hospital and advised his village helpers to return home and continue their education. Many of the women, who had accepted responsibility and experienced the thrill of meaningful work, were unwilling to return to traditional roles. They asked instead to remain. Chowdhury, himself, gave up the idea of returning to his earlier life. The war had brought him face to face with realities that had formerly been mere statistics, and he recognized that an advanced degree in surgery was irrelevant to the work that needed to be done in his homeland.

Bangladesh, among the world's poorest nations, was also among the most densely populated. Its citizenry was predominately rural, illiterate and conservative. Existing health facilities were inadequate, both in quantity and quality, and modern hospitals and medical personnel were concentrated in the urban areas and accessible to only the privileged few. In the countryside malaria, tuberculosis, smallpox, diptheria, tetanus and whooping cough were endemic, and malnutrition among children was common.

Soon after cessation of hostilities Chowdhury tried to explain his ideas for rural health to government and non-governmental organizations, and to the World Health Organization (WHO) of the United Nations. He advocated a campaign of massive inoculations and instruction in family planning techniques, employing young veterans of the liberation struggle as paramedics.

He also proposed to delay reopening the universities for one year, arguing that the young (like his 14 year old brother who had helped blow up bridges) could hardly be expected to become schoolboys again overnight. He suggested they be asked instead to help rebuild the country, for only then would they realize that construction is more difficult than destruction.

The government rejected his radical ideas, but gave him a house in Dhaka for a hospital. He and three other doctors moved in, accompanied by some 40 young nurses and paramedics who had elected to stay. Chowdhury knew the capital was not the place to start implementing his ideas, but the building enabled him to keep staff and equipment together and allowed him time to organize for an eventual shift to the countryside.

Two months later the young doctor received a gift from a private donor of approximately one hectare—later increased to three and a half—in Savar, 40 kilometers north of Dhaka. The location was ideal for a pilot project: there was no hospital in the population area of 170,000, the literacy rate was low, and the site was near the capital. The last he knew was important because, for a demonstration facility to be effective, it must be readily accessible to decision makers.

Chowdhury moved his hospital to Savar in April and registered it as a nongovernmental charitable trust and a voluntary organization dedicated to the promotion of rural health and community development. He initially held meetings with the villagers to determine the best method of bringing medical services to them, and eventually adopted the idea of a hospital center and a number of sub-centers.

Chowdhury named the hospital Gonoshasthaya Kendra (GK, People's Health Center). The name has an intentionally socialist ring to it. Chowdhury did not want to found just another rural health program or philanthropic enterprise, but a project whose underlying philosophy emphasized human equality, individual worth and the dignity of labor. Equality was to be a precept for guiding all undertakings.

Chowdhury's ideas were sound and his faith in the good sense and integrity of the common man was rewarded. Gonoshasthaya Kendra prospered and grew. Today GK employs over two hundred workers and includes a hospital, a medical outreach program, an insurance plan, a school, a farm, living quarters for workers and vocational training centers. The complex is managed by a board of directors, but major issues are decided by workers at monthly meetings presided over by an elected chairman.

The 20-bed hospital staffed by eight doctors, two of whom were trained in the U.S. and one in England, is the heart of the complex. Its beds are reserved for serious cases or emergencies. GK has resisted the urge to enlarge the hospital; instead it emphasizes outpatient treatment which is less costly. Moreover, Chowdhury insists a patient recovers faster at home where the diet is familiar and the care more personal. The hospital is, however, equipped with a modern operating theater and sophisticated diagnostic intruments and is "home base" for the five health centers that together service a rural area of 250,000 people. Each center has a five-bed ward and is in turn headquarters for GK paramedics in the region. GK doctors take turns staffing the centers, but a senior paramedic is in charge of each; some 120 paramedics, divided between Savar and the centers, bear the burden of the medical work. The paramedics are actually better trained for the simple medical and surgical work they perform than the doctors, who have often learned more theory and advanced technology than routine practical medicine. And, since the social/educational gap is not as great, the paramedics have more rapport with their village patients.

Most of the paramedics are women. To provide women an opportunity of earning a living, and to prove his theory that the Bangladesh economy will develop only with their participation, Chowdhury gives women employment preference in all GK operations. "When you talk of poverty," he reminds listeners, "you are talking about women. In this country poor women are twice oppressed: first because they are poor, and second because they are women." He is convinced that progress will occur only if tradition—both the cruel cause and the tragic result of this waste of female talent—can be broken.

The hold of tradition, however, is strong. A survey in 1974 among Bangladeshi farmers revealed that the majority advocated female marriage before age 15 as a deterrent to sexual offenses. But the reality for girls of such an early union is a quarter century of childbearing. Another burden faced by women is the threat of divorce should they fail to produce a male heir. "Once divorced," Chowdhury points out, "a woman would not be accepted by her parents to whom she would only be another mouth to feed. Neither could she find employment to support herself. She could choose. As a beggar she could go to town and there discard the last shred of any human dignity she may have had, or she could take the more attractive way of insecticide poisoning." Should a husband die or become infirm, his wife's fate would be equally gloomy.[1]

In keeping with his concern for women the paramedics trained at GK are mostly rural women between the ages of 17 and 25. Their greatest strength is their understanding of village life. They live and work in areas where 70 percent of the people die without a doctor, where potable water may be a distant walk, and where human waste is excreted in a corner of the family plot.

Not all aides receive full paramedic training. The most elementary course is given to the *dai* (midwives), usually illiterate women who have learned their craft as apprentices. Their instruction, lasting only one week, is designed to fill gaps in their basic knowledge. For example, Chowdhury says: "I ask them, 'When do you wash your hands?' 'After holding the baby and cutting the cord,' they answer. Then I tell them that for half a million *taka* (US$18,436) I learned in medical school to wash my hands *before* and to put the thread and blade into hot water."[2] After covering basic hygiene he teaches them to treat common ailments and introduces them to family planning techniques. They receive a monthly supplement from GK of Tk.50.

The second group, also illiterate, is trained by GK for the government. The women receive one month of instruction on

1. "Zafrullah Chowdhury," *The Ramon Magsaysay Awards 1985–1987*. Manila: Magsaysay Award Foundation. To be published 1990.
2. *Ibid.*

the treatment of common ailments—diarrhea, skin diseases, intestinal parasites, burns, shock and poisoning—and they attend lectures where family planning is fully discussed. After returning to their villages they will be evaluated by a GK doctor or advanced paramedic and will return to Savar for further training twice within the next 18 months. The government pays them a stipend of Tk.100 a month.

The third category comprises GK's own paramedics. With rare exception they are required to have five years of schooling and be literate. Their training lasts from six months to a year. "Lectures stressing the relationship between poverty and disease take a big chunk out of our curriculum," Chowdhury laments, "but they must understand these things." They are also taught how to treat the most prevalent diseases (70 percent of the caseload); how to do blood, urine, sputum and stool tests; and how to perform female sterilization.

The preferred method of female sterilization is the mini-laparotomy, an operation introduced by Dr. Vittoon Osathanondh, a Thai population expert. The method is so simple that the paramedics have performed over 7,000 successful operations with an infection rate lower than in similar operations performed by physicians—probably because the more complicated cases are handled by the latter.

Chowdhury was initially discouraged from attempts to popularize family planning in rural areas: a friendly government official warned him that his paramedics would be physically beaten. But a chance encounter with some village women proved the bureaucrat wrong and dispelled Chowdhury's fears for his young helpers' safety. The village women said they were seeking "the doctor from England who might know how to stop having babies." From that day on the promotion of family planning has been a major effort of each paramedic.

In Chowdhury's view early government attempts at curbing the birth rate—largely financed and influenced by foreign aid organizations—were misdirected and inadequate. Contraceptive pills or devices were given without adequate instructions, and when pills were consumed in improper dose and caused harmful side effects, the women understandably stopped taking them. Moreover, foreign-supported clinics often offered cash or rice to women who accepted sterilization. Chowdhury views this bribing of unsophisticated and illiterate women as forced sterilization and a possible threat to their well-being, since young wives are known to have been forced by husbands or mothers-in-law to accept sterilization for the food or cash payment, and then discarded on the grounds that they were no longer fertile. GK paramedics not only charge for contraceptives (so they will not be taken carelessly or wasted) and sterilization, but refuse to sterilize a woman unless she has at least two living sons.

In the beginning female paramedics were hampered by the distance of Savar from the sub-centers. Their male counterparts shortened their journeys by bicycling, but a cultural taboo forced the women to walk. No amount of urging on Chowdhury's part could induce them to change.

One day a break came. A student, who was about to be expelled, begged for one more chance. "Only if you learn to ride a bicycle," Chowdhury countered. She agreed and was soon pedaling around the compound. Other girls, envious of her skill, learned also, yet none was willing to venture outside the GK gates for fear of harassment.

Finally the day came when four girls rode to work. Their route was through an orthodox Muslim village where they were seen by the horrified townfolk. The men, incensed at this breach of propriety, accosted Chowdhury saying:

"Doctor, you did a very bad thing. Girls on bicycles! God will not forgive them, and we will catch them on their way back and punish them."

Instead of answering the men directly, Chowdhury turned to the headman and inquired about his mother's eye operation in Dhaka.

"How did she go, Haji Sahib, did she walk?"

"Oh, you must be joking, Doctor. You cannot walk 40 kilometers. We took a bus."

"Was the bus empty?" Chowdhury asked.

"Oh no, it was quite full," the headman admitted.

"Do not tell me, Haji Sahib, that your mother went in a crowded bus with men *touching* her on all sides? At least our girls on bicycles are not *touched* by men!"[3]

---

3. *Ibid.*

Henceforth women paramedics visited their patients on bicycles with few onlookers daring to criticize.

The following year one young woman suggested the women celebrate May Day—a major socialist holiday—by cycling to Dhaka. Twenty-three agreed. The press was alerted and a reception awaited them when they pedaled into the capital. Their exploit made newspaper headlines and caught the eye of the nation's president, who knew how wasteful to society are taboos against women. He thereupon ordered bicycles for *all* government health workers. The GK project later became a blueprint for the government's rural health program.

The salaries of paramedics, like those of every other GK employee, are decided at GK mass meetings, where voting is by show of hands and the marjoity rules. The paramedics also receive fringe benefits in the familiar industrial sense: housing, schooling for their children, subsidized dining facilities and medical insurance.

Medical insurance is an innovative feature of GK. An applicant is assigned to one of three categories. Category A is for the poorest, defined as a family which forgoes meals during some part of the year. Category B is for those who, although poor, never starve; and Category C for the rich, i.e., farmers with a surplus.

Category A families are exempt from membership fee, but pay Tk.1 (US$.04) for each consultation; this slight charges covers the cost of all subsequent treatment and prescription drugs. Members of Category B pay an annual membership fee of Tk.10, and Tk.2 per head per consultation. The consultation fee includes medicine, but additional fees are charged for x-rays or an operation. Category C members pay Tk.20 per year, Tk.5 per visit, and higher fees for other services. Everyone, regardless of category, must pay for family planning devices and abortions. When hospitalization is unavoidable, those in Category A pay one *taka* per day, in B three and in C five.

Currently 60,000 persons are enrolled at Savar alone. Subscription fees and consultation charges cover from 50 to 60 percent of the hospital operating costs. In the past bank loans and grants from NOVIB (Nederlandse Organisatie voor Ontwikkelingssamenwerking) covered the deficit. Now profits from

Gonoshasthaya Pharmaceuticals (see below) are expected to make up the difference.

Although not all GK employees enroll their children, Chowdhury operates a five-year school within the GK complex. Like most GK projects it is experimental and a radical departure from tradition. A 1976 survey in Bangladesh revealed that only 54 percent of the nation's children attended school. Of those who did, only 14 percent of the girls and 33 percent of the boys completed five grades, the minimum for literacy. Many peasants found education a drawback. A literate boy might seek a living in the city and be lost to the family as a farmhand, thereby increasing the burden of the rest of the family. And it was difficult to find a husband for an educated girl: no unschooled boy would want her and dowries for literate bridegrooms were costly. Moreover, many parents felt they could not spare their children from routine rural chores.

Although peasants consider education a luxury, Chowdhury considers it a necessity if the villager hopes to avoid exploitation. Every peasant who signs a contract or loan with his thumbprint, he points out, is in danger of being cheated. He thus fashioned his school to fit the perceived needs of the villagers. Since children are needed for harvest the GK school is closed at such times. As farm children must also care for siblings and tend animals, students are allowed to bring younger brothers and sisters into the classroom and graze their animals with the GK herd. Since children of the poorest families are often sent out as servants or other menials at a nominal wage, teachers point out to parents that the small wage lost while attending school is partially compensated for by the free meal provided each student. (Food, the school's biggest budget item, is variously provided for by Australian Community Aid Abroad and by rice donations from the local government.)

The school curriculum emphasizes reading and writing in Bengali and introduces a few useful English words and some basic mathematics. An innovation is the pupil-teacher program: quick learners are assigned to tutor slower learners or conduct afternoon literacy classes in the village for adults or school dropouts. The young tutors are not paid for their work; their incentive is pride. In the Savar area there are now 15 afternoon classes, meeting in courtyards or under a tree. The GK class-room itself is not much more elaborate. It is of bamboo and mud construction, like the village houses, and students sit on the mud floor.

The success of the school, however, has been impressive. The normal student retention rate is 90 percent, compared to 15 percent in government schools, and 30 percent of the most recent graduates have gone on to high school. Functional literacy classes, primarily for women, are also taught. These emphasize learning to read simple directions and measurements and understand the economics of production.

From the schoolhouse windows one looks directly onto the eight hectare farm. Chowdhury had insisted a farm be an integral part of the GK complex, since Bangladesh is an agricultural country, with 70 percent of its GNP so generated. The country cannot be understood or its problems solved, he believes, unless its agricultural economy is addressed sympathetically. Therefore everyone, including doctors and staff, begins each workday with one hour of agricultural activity. In this way all, regardless of background, have some understanding of the problems of farming and of the rural poor. The benefit of regular physical activity is a happy byproduct.

Not all appreciate this policy, and mandatory labor is one reason staff leave. Farm work has also been a source of friction between farmers and the professionals. A complaint often heard at monthly meetings is that doctors shirk their vegetable patch chores, even though they (including Chowdhury) are given "simple jobs" such as planting and weeding. The complicated agricultural tasks are left to the farmers. Women are involved in fieldwork—as well as in traditional agricultural occupations that usually take place within a family compound—in order to refute the prevalent notion "that women do not participate in agricultural output." Milk cattle, chickens and ducks are raised, besides fruits, vegetables and rice. The output is bought for use in the communal dining hall and any surplus is sold in the village. The land is so fertile that it can produce five crops a year.

Although apartments are provided rent-free for GK workers, dining hall meals, electricity and other amenities are charged for on a sliding scale. An avowed socialist, Chowdhury believes that those earning more should pay more. He, as a physician, earns Tk.3,000 per month. He therefore pays Tk.400 each for himself and his wife Susan—a West German volunteer at his field hospital whom he married in 1972—and Tk. 200 for Brishti, their 12 year old daughter. A paramedic who earns Tk.600 pays only Tk.150. Apartments are assigned on the basis of family size. Chowdhury has a one-bedroom apartment for his family of three; a workman with four children is allotted three bedrooms.

Within the GK compound more than a dozen small manufacturing shops produce a variety of goods. All make money, but profit is not the principal motive. The shops were set up as vocational training centers so villagers could learn skills such as welding, carpentry, weaving and baking, and augment their incomes.

GK also operates a small printing plant that publishes *Mashik Gonoshasthaya* (People's Health Monthly), featuring articles on family problems, women's issues and various aspects of exploitation. It sells for Tk.5 and has a circulation of 20,000 throughout Bangladesh and the border districts of India.

Chowdhury has long been involved in an attack on the high cost and proliferation of medicinal drugs, marketed primarily by multinational pharmaceutical companies. Ironically, studies show that poor nations and individuals pay proportionately more for medicines than do the rich. In Bangladesh, for example, about 40 percent of the total health budget is spent on drugs; in contrast Britain spends only 10 percent. In the case of individuals, where doctors are few the poor rely heavily on over-the-counter remedies. Druggists, seldom qualified, push expensive medication, and misleading advertisements by drug companies lure the unsophisticated into wasting money on useless medicines which can often be harmful if taken incorrectly.

About one-third of the drugs marketed by multinationals in Bangladesh and other developing countries are vitamins and tonics, another 15 percent have been banned in some developed countries. Although vitamins, tonics and elixirs rarely kill, they can be addictive as well as expensive; one popular vitamin tonic for example, contains 27.5 percent alcohol. Improper drug usage is particularly prevalent in Bangladesh because women are in seclusion and husbands and fathers buy remedies by merely describing their wives' or children's symptoms to druggists, who in turn recommend whatever they feel appropriate and within the purchaser's budget.

In 1977 WHO published *The Selection of Essential Drugs,* which was updated and reissued in 1982. It advised Third World nations to restrict the import, manufacture and use of drugs to about 225 items. It pointed out that dysenteric illnesses, tetanus, malaria and respiratory infections are the major killers in poor countries; the prevalance of these diseases can be drastically reduced by the introduction of clean water, sanitation and good nutrition—and treated by a few simple medicines. WHO Director General Dr. Halfdan Mahler suggested that "for the villager and urban slum dweller great miracles could be achieved with fewer than 30 well-chosen drugs." Yet in 1980 in Bangladesh over 4,000 different drugs were on pharmacy shelves or on peddlers' mats.

In 1979 Chowdhury, in consultation with Jan Willem van der Eb of the Netherlands, and aided by grants from NOVIB, OXFAM and Christian Aid, began a factory at Savar to produce low cost generic drugs. Gonoshasthaya Pharmaceuticals Ltd. is organized as other manufacturing companies, with two major differences. It has no individual shareholders but is 100 percent owned by the Gonoshasthaya Kendra Charitable Trust; and its charter requires that 50 percent of its profits be invested in factory expansion, with the balance used to finance other GK projects and programs.

The company is pledged to produce essential, high quality drugs at reasonable prices, and operates on four principles: keeping the public up-to-date concerning harmful effects and misuse of medication; opposing drug sales on credit because credit encourages unnecessary purchases; preventing a few distributors from monopolizing Gonoshasthaya products; and refusing to push slow moving items.

Skepticism initially greeted the new enterprise, but Chowdhury and his colleagues never doubted its success. Once production started even they were astonished to discover how cheap it was to produce the average drug. They could, for example, make a five milligram tablet of Diajapam (Valium) for three *paisa* (*paisa* is a 20th of a *taka*), sell it at five *paisa* and make a 20 percent profit. The same tablet was being sold by others for Tk.1 (almost seven times as much). The company takes a lower profit on essential drugs and a higher one on those less critical, but its overall profit is 15 percent after operating costs, depreciation and taxes. To prove the accuracy of his pricing and the quality of his product Chowdhury invited the Minister of Health to look at his books and inspect the factory. The minister, himself a doctor, was astounded.

Gonoshasthaya Pharmaceuticals is a fully modern plant, among Bangladesh's largest, with 3,906 square meters of floor space. Quality control, equipment maintenance, airconditioning and humidity control all meet international standards. Superficially there is little to distinguish it from other well-run factories. But unlike its capitalist counterparts, the plant operates on the philosophy common to all GK projects: women are given job preference, training is provided the rural poor, daily agricultural work is mandatory, and profit is not the primary motive. For example, although the plant has a high-speed machine capable of packing thousands of capsules per hour, it is seldom used because it displaces several workers. The preferred machine is an older, slower one which requires four women to operate. The modern machine is on hand only to fill government orders which are usually large and urgently needed.

By 1982 Gonoshasthaya Pharmaceuticals was producing affordable, quality drugs, but 10 multinationals still controlled 75 percent of the market and still sold medicines that WHO deemed nonessential; the rural poor still bought packaged preparations from illiterate, and even blind, peddlars. A national policy controlling the import and sale of drugs was clearly needed—as Chowdhury had tried to prove to every government for the past eight years.

To his surprise, therefore, and within days of the March 24, 1982 coup by Lieutenant-General Hossain Mohammad Ershad, Chowdhury was asked to help formulate a new drug policy. As he was a doctor, ran a successful pharmaceutical firm, understood the medical needs of rural Bangladesh, and had long written, lectured and lobbied for such a change, the government's choice was logical. But Chowdhury at first refused to believe that a military government, in debt to foreign donors, could pioneer the radical measures he advocated: he believed only a socialist government could implement such a policy. Finally convinced of the government's sincerity, he agreed to cooperate, despite his own misgivings and the warning of his friends.

Consequently one month after the coup Chowdhury joined seven other experts on the newly-formed Drug (Control) Committee, appointed to draw up policy recommendations. Multinational corporations lodged objections with the government— which the government ignored—and the group began its deliberations.

The committee worked in secret, often 18 hours a day, and produced a report the second week in May. One month later, on June 12, 1982, the government promulgated the committee's recommendations as the Drug (Control) Ordinance.

The committee's report argued that drugs are essential tools for health care so must be treated differently from other commercial products. It recommended that 1,700 unnecessary drugs be phased out, and it proposed safeguarding and promoting the local drug industry by prohibiting multinationals from manufacturing or importing products locally available, or of simple formulation which require no special machinery or technical expertise.

The report recommended specific drugs (by generic name) for the three levels of the government health program: 12 drugs were listed for the village level, an additional 33 for sub-centers, and another 105 for the central health clinics. A supplemental list of 100 drugs was suggested for use by specialists.

Reaction, as expected, was mixed. Many foreign governments, organizations and individuals wrote or cabled their congratulations. The Asian Development Bank called the recommendations "steps in the right direction." But the home governments of multinationals—notably the United States, United Kingdom and West Germany, all important aid donors— urged the Bangladesh government to reconsider.

The national medical association, many of whose members were Western-trained, initially criticized the policy as precipitous, but later reversed itself. The multinationals, on the other hand, launched an advertising campaign accusing Chowdhury,

War on Want and OXFAM of conspiracy. Other than agreeing to form a review committee which suggested some modifications that were accepted, the government remained steadfast in the face of the controversy which raged for months.

Eventually the success of the policy muted opposition. The English-language *Bangladesh Observer* in March 1985 reported: "With the implementation of the new drug policy 1,707 harmful and unnecessary drugs have been banned. The new drug policy has saved *takas* 30 *crore* (US$1,106,000) in foreign exchange and encouraged local pharmaceutical companies to meet the country's requirements."

Chowdhury is still far from satisfied with the Bangladesh health system, and ways to improve it are very much on his mind. He wants a law passed that would require the use of generic names on the 45 essential drugs marketed for village and sub-center usage, and he is agitating for a regulation to force multinationals to engage in the transfer of technology.

He is also engaged in building a medical school near Savar which emphasizes rural holistic medicine, an institution where doctors "will be trained for health, not for disease." Like all GK projects, this is intended as a model which he hopes the government will copy.

Ideologically, Chowdhury is still a dedicated socialist but he belongs to no political organization. It is his own brand of practical, down-to-earth socialism that has given birth to the GK philosophy and is the magnet which pulls professional and management staff to Savar.

In the course of his numerous activities Chowdhury has achieved international stature. Recognition of his accomplishments came first in Europe, where in 1974 he received the Swedish Youth Prize. Four years later his own nation conferred on him its prestigious Independence Day Award, and in 1981, the Maulana Bhasani Award for his efforts in health and family planning. The 1985 Magsaysay Community Leadership Award recognized him for engineering "Bangladesh's new drug policy, eliminating unnecessary pharmaceuticals, and making comprehensive medical care more available to ordinary citizens." The citation might have added: for emphasizing "the worth of the individual, the dignity of labor and the rights and necessary role of women in rural society."

Credit for the Rural Poor

Muhammad Yunus

In most villages throughout the Third World inadequate access to reasonable credit remains a major hurdle to the fulfillment of basic human aspirations. The interest on investment or consumption loans in Bangladesh, for example, can be as high as 120 percent per annum, and complex application procedures and lack of collateral can create almost insurmountable impediments. Access to credit favors those who already hold wealth or exercise power.

The problem is compounded by myths concerning the poor: they cannot save, they will not work together, they have no marketable skills and they are uninterested or fearful of change. The life of the poor is thus seen as an unbreakable, self-perpetuating cycle of poverty, with the high population growth rate exacerbating their already overwhelming misery.

Muhammad Yunus disagrees with this popular view. As an economist he believes that poverty is not caused by a person's unwillingness to work or his lack of skill. A poor person may work very hard, even harder than others, but the poor man languishes in poverty because he is not paid full worth for his work; under the existing social and economic institutional arrangements a middleman skims off the major portion of the income due him.

If the self-employed poor could gradually build up an asset-base, Yunus reasoned, they could command a greater share of their productive efforts. Since credit is a liquid asset, the recipient of credit could decide how and where to build his asset-base. With assets thus at his disposal, an individual would be free, or at least freer, to build his own fate with his own labor.

Muhammad Yunus was born on June 28, 1940 in Chittagong, Bengal, which was still part of India. His father, Muhammad Dula Meah, was a prosperous gold and jewelry merchant whose limited education and deep religious beliefs never prevented him from encouraging Yunus and his brothers to study, travel and experience new things. His mother, Sufia Khatun, had little education, but was a highly intelligent woman who also encouraged her son to see and think for himself.

Placing first in citywide fourth grade exams, young Yunus transferred to the prestigious Chittagong Middle English School, where he placed first in his class despite the fact his earlier schooling was not in English.

At 15 he travelled as a Pakistani representative to the Boy Scouts World Jamboree in Canada, and became convinced from his experiences at that early age that human nature is everywhere the same. This belief was reinforced by his six-month tour of Europe and the Middle East which followed, and by later trips to the Philippines and Japan.

Yunus returned from his Canadian trip to enter Chittagong College in mid-term. He chose to follow an arts instead of science program, much to the bewilderment of his advisors: all the other bright students took science to prepare themselves to become doctors or engineers. He also expanded his extracurricular activities by singlehandedly producing a small paper, and continued in this vein when he entered Dhaka University (1957), founding and co-editing a nationally circulated literary magazine called *Uttaran* (Advancement).

Receiving his B.A. (Honors in Economics) in 1960, and his M.A. the following year, Yunus returned to Chittagong College to teach economics, at the same time setting up a commercial printing business in partnership with his father. But the young teacher soon realized that he was spending more time than he wanted to on this venture; he also realized that, since his ambition was to teach in a university, he needed a Ph.D. Therefore he turned the business over to his father and an elder brother, and applied for and received a Fulbright Scholarship to study "development economics" at Vanderbilt University in Nashville, Tennessee.

Yunus had completed his Ph.D., and was teaching economics at Tennessee State University, when he learned that the Pakistan Army had taken control of Dhaka (March 1971) to try to control the rapidly deteriorating policital situation in East Pakistan. Like Zafrullah Chowdhury and Fazle Hasan Abed, he immediately became an activist for the Bengal separatist cause.

With five other Bengalis living in Nashville Yunus formed the Bangladesh Citizens' Committee, and later moved to Washington D.C. where he manned the Bangladesh Information Center and began to lobby the U.S. Congress and foreign embassies for diplomatic recognition of his newly proclaimed nation. He helped raised funds to send non-military equipment to Bangladeshi forces, published a newsletter under the aegis of the Bangladesh Defense League, and with others created the Bangladesh Emergency Fund to raise money for relief work. As soon as possible after the "liberation" of Bangladesh he returned to Dhaka to see how he could best serve his new nation.

However, finding the government in disarray and the jobs offered him meaningless, Yunus disappointedly returned to his family home in Chittagong. There the University of Chittagong offered him the position of Chairman of the Department of Economics.

In addition to academic ability and experience, the young professor brought to his job ideas about practical research, an unfulfilled desire to do something for his country, and a belief that gradualism is the only feasible way to achieve lasting change.

The opportunity to act upon his ideas and beliefs lay at hand. Just outside the campus was the tiny village of Jobra. It was December when Yunus saw it, and the land was barren, but neighboring areas were green and fertile. He inquired of the villagers why their land was lying idle. They looked at him in astonishment. It's the dry season, they patiently explained; the other areas can plant during the dry season because they have tubewells for irrigation. Yunus determined to obtain a tubewell for Jobra.

Yunus felt a personal concern about this village because, as he has said, "a university is a reservoir of knowledge for the whole world, and if that knowledge doesn't spill over to the nearest land, then it is useless." After a year of applying at one government agency after the other, he finally convinced the Bangladesh Agricultural Development Corporation to provide the needed tubewell.

The results were far from satisfactory. In the first year of operation the villagers planted only three and a half hectares during the dry season; in the second year four; and in the third year none! All government information on tubewells had indicated that once a tubewell was sunk, productivity would increase enormously. Why, he asked himself, had this not happened?

Instead of being discouraged Yunus decided Jobra offered an excellent case-study for the students of his Rural Economics Program, the first course offered in Bangladesh which focused equally on class work and field research. Calling a public meeting between the students and villagers to discuss the situation, he and the students received a lesson in village politics. The tubewell was not being utilized, the villagers explained, because of the tensions it had created within the village.

Each person using the well was supposed to pay his share for the diesel fuel to operate the pump, however some used the well without paying, and others claimed they had paid but received no water. Those few who continued to use the well had suffered so much from infighting that after two years they had given up; the whole village agreed the government should remove it.

Yunus suggested an alternative that he called the Tebhaga Khamar (three-share farm) plan. The plan called for choosing a committee which would supply each farmer with as much water, rice seed and fertilizer as he needed. At harvest time the farmer would divide his harvest into three: one-third for the landlord, one-third for himself, and one-third for the committee which would have borrowed money to provide the necessary inputs. The committee would then sell its share of the rice, pay back the money borrowed, and finance the next crop. If there was a surplus the committee would share it among the farmers who had participated in the plan.

The villagers were doubtful; they were interested in the possibility of profit, but wanted no part of a loss. Yunus, therefore, offered to take personal responsibility for a loss, emphasizing he was doing so because he was certain the plan would work. The villagers acquiesced. The landlords agreed to accept one-third of the crop as called for by the plan, instead of their ususal half; Yunus insisted on a written agreement so there could be no reneging at harvest time. He then arranged for a personal loan of 65,000 *takas* from a commercial bank to cover initial operating costs.

The original plan called for irrigating only 16 hectares the first year (even though the tubewell was supposed to be able to supply 32) since Jobra's soil was very porous and Yunus wanted to be certain the project would succeed. Thus when the number of hectares to be cultivated snowballed to 34, he warned the committee there might not be enough water. The members shrugged. For only Tk.1,000 more, they said, they could put a crossdam in a local stream which would flood the fields and provide the extra water needed—an option that had always been available to them but never acted upon!

The dam was built, the crop was harvested and the yield tripled from 27 *maunds* (1 *maund* equals 40 kg) per hectare to 82; the national average was 42. Everyone was pleased with the results except Yunus. When he went to get the money to repay his bank loan, he learned the committee had not collected enough rice to cover the debt. The landlords had received their share, presumably because they were present during every day of harvest; the farmers had taken their share and apparently could not resist taking part of the committee's third. It was his own fault, the committe said unconcernedly, because he had not been on hand to protect his interests; he had trusted the people too much.

Yunus used his own money to repay the bank and chalked the loss up to experience, but when the villagers asked him to obtain a loan to finance the next harvest, he refused. Instead he gave the committee advice on the lending process, introduced them to the banker and insisted they handle the financing themselves.

The committe did so and devised a fool-proof system for collecting its share of the next harvest: the farmers were required to bring all of the grain to the committee yard, and give the committee its share before they could take out their own.

This time the Tebhaga Khamar project was so successful that the committee was able to buy an electric motor for the tubewell to replace the diesel engine, greatly reducing operating costs because the village was already electrified. The crossdam was maintained, saving enough water to irrigate twice the expected area. And the committee went on to purchase its own land and build godowns for storage and husking. Each year the profits have increased.

What Yunus learned from the Jobra experiment became the basis of his approach to rural development:

1. Solutions are not self-fulfilling.

2. Recipients must be involved deeply enough to give their full support and work to capacity.

3. Local problems should be solved by the community; often solutions are known but have not been acted upon.

4. Local organizations are most effective when they develop their own structure and rules.

5. Attention must always be given to class structure so the wealthiest and most powerful do not control a program to the detriment of the poor.

Yunus also learned in the course of his research in the villages that the people most receptive to new ideas are those who have the least to lose—the landless poor, those who sell their labor to survive. Since they are not tied to the land, they are mobile, enterprising and open to new ideas. Moreover, he disovered to his shock, they were rapidly increasing in numbers. Landlessness had risen in Bengal in the "recent past" from 18 to 40 or 50 percent! When questioned, the local villagers who were landless indicated that 252 families of them had become landless in their own lifetimes, compared to 89 in their fathers' and 18 in their grandfathers'.

When Yunus published the results of his Tebhaga Khamar project the government expressed interest, eventually borrowing the idea and renaming it the Package Input Program (PIP). The government ordered banks all over the country to provide loans for similar enterprises. In 1978 Tebhaga Khamar in Jobra received the President's Award for introducing innovative organization in agriculture.

Unfortunately none of the government PIPs developed a sustained, successful operation. There had been no arrangements made for village participation in decision making; the program had been decreed from above, with a poor understanding of the concept both by officials and recipients.

This did not surprise Yunus, who as early as 1974 had tried to convince his fellow economists and the government that local problems should be handled at a local level where they were best understood, and that massive government structure imposed from the top does not work. He advocated a form of village government (*gram sarkar*) be formed, responsible for village needs—food, employment, health and literacy—and consisting of 10 representative members: two landless poor, two well-to-do farmers, two women, two youths, and two from the professions. The head of the government should be elected directly by all the villagers and thus be responsible to all.

Urging the need for such new strategies and local institutions, Yunus used the example of food shortages to illustrate his position. No results, he pointed out, are gained from the Food Minister appearing on national television, stating that there is a 2,500,000-ton food shortage, and appealing for citizen help. The villager who cannot count has no conception of 2,500,000 tons; he therefore dismisses the problem, being sure that it is beyond his ability to resolve. When the problem is approached at the village level, however, it becomes manageable. A villager knows how much extra rice needs to be grown to provide for the marginal or starving in his own community.

Yunus also feels that little effect is achieved by donations of food from abroad. Foreign aid, he says, trickles down "about half an inch," when it needs to "trickle down a mile to reach those for whom it is intended and who really need it."

Conversely, Yunus recognizes that people and institutions often exhaust their energies seeking national government aid, when local initiative can frequently provide the necessary input (e.g. the crossdam), and concurrently foster pride and self-reliance, rather than dependency.

In 1975 President Zia Ur Rahman became convinced that *gram sarkar,* like Yunus' earlier program, Tebhaga Khanar, was a suitable pattern for village governments nationwide. Unfortunately he chose to create them by government decree, rather than by encouraging villages to develop their own organizations, with the national government providing help and support only when needed. Although some *gram sarkars* were successful, most survived in name only; when Zia was assasinated in 1981 they were abolished by the new regime.

The convention, in 1976, of the Bangladesh Economics Association had proposed for its next meeting the topic "Self-Reliance for the Rural Poor." The subject interested Yunus but he publicly doubted that any proposals from academicians or government economists would be effective. He pointed out two problems: the definition of "poor," and the fact that no one at the convention, including himself, had any real knowledge of the poor and how they lived.

The international definition of poor had usually been "a small or marginal farmer," but in the context of Bangladesh, a small farmer was comparatively well-off. The automatic connection between the words "poor" and "farmer" was also incorrect Yunus argued. Not only are most of the truly poor landless, but 50 percent of them are women and thus totally ignored.

He was bothered, too, by the accepted canon that the poor make no contribution to society, that they are takers rather than producers, and lack skills. Nevertheless statistics on caloric intake and per capita income indicated the poor were exhibiting surprising survival skills and were in fact multiplying. Their skills should be supported and encouraged, he reasoned, and even if their individual input was very small, in view of their great numbers their effect could well be enormous.

Determined to learn more about the poor in Jobra, Yunus sent two students from his Rural Economics Program into the village to find out how many families had a supply of food for: 1) one year, 2) six months, 3) one month, and 4) how many lived from hand to mouth? Once this data was assembled, the researchers were sent back to concentrate on those whose lives were eked out on a day-to-day basis. These desperately poor, they confirmed, were primarily women who performed many jobs during the year but received little profit from their labor. For example, one woman who wove bamboo stools had to borrow the money to purchase bamboo from the same trader who bought her stools. By the time he deducted the amount of her loan from the price of her stools she was left with two cents for a full day's work.

Yunus then asked the students to find out how much capita would be needed to make these women independent, i.e. able to purchase outright their raw materials so they could sell their finished products to the highest bidder, rather than the trader who held their debt. The students discovered that the 42 women in the village who fit the criteria needed only a total of Tk.850: the highest amount one person needed was Tk.65, the lowest about Tk.10. Incredibly, these women were forced into permanent indebtedness for sums as little as US$0.80!

The first inclination of Yunus was to lend them money himself, but he knew he could not go on doing so indefinitely. Who, he asked rhetorically, should be lending them money? The obvious answer was the banks. Therefore he approached the campus branch of the Janata Bank from which he had borrowed money for the Tebhaga Khamar experiment, and asked if the bank would make small loans to poor villagers who lacked collateral. The manager was firm. His job, he said, was to take in money, not to give loans: the latter was the responsibility of the main office in Chittagong which had approved the earlier loan.

Yunus called at the Chittagong office and explained his ideas. The manager was agreeable, provided a well-to-do villager would underwrite each loan. Since this would be tantamount to bondaging each poor borrower to a rich lender, Yunus rejected the offer, but seized on the concept of underwriting. He offered to co-sign any number of loans but told the manager, frankly, that he had no intention of paying if anyone defaulted; if there was a problem the bank would have to take him to court. Surprisingly the manager accepted this condition and agreed to provide the financing he requested.

The first money was made available by Janata Bank in December 1976 to what became the Grameen Bank Prakalpa (GBP, Village Bank Project). Borrowers were from the lowest income group, the landless poor; full repayment was expected, and a large percentage of the borrowers were women. Remembering his experience in the Tebhaga Khamar program, Yunus took great pains to organize his new project carefully to forestall any expensive mistakes.

In the four years he had been involved with Jobra, Yunus had gained considerable insight into the psychology of villagers. He understood their wariness of institutions, so all GBP transactions were carried out in the village square, rather than in the formal atmosphere of a bank. GBP workers were required to be seen in the village, answering questions and collecting payments. Yunus also understood that quirk of human nature which prompts a borrower to repay small amounts on a regular basis, but makes the same borrower reluctant to repay a large sum at one time. Thus he decided that borrowers would pay back roughly two percent of their loan each week.

Most importantly Yunus had learned the value of group dynamics at the village level. A group, he recognized, provides support and encouragement to its members, as well as constant monitoring, and a small group is preferable to a large one. In small groups there is little opportunity for dissembling or laziness; responsibility is clearly delineated. Yunus therefore decided that loans would be made only to individuals who belong to a group of an optimum size of five. Each member of the group must want a loan, must understand the loan process and must be willing to cooperate. No one in the group can own more than one-sixth of a hectare nor be closely related to another group member.

Once the group has chosen a leader and discussed the business proposition involved in each loan, it approaches a bank worker who makes sure members understand the repayment process and can sign their names. Initially two members are allowed to borrow. They begin their new businesses and start their weekly repayments under the watchful eyes of the other members. If, after two months, the two are working hard and making their repayments, a second two are permitted to borrow. The fifth member only receives his or her loan after a further two months. Each borrower has up to a year to repay his loan;

he then begins to repay the interest on the loan, which is calculated at normal bank rates.

The groups, in turn, are required to join with other groups to form a Center, choose a mutually convenient time for required weekly meetings, and elect a chief and deputy who assume responsibility for the financial conduct of all Center members. Bank workers conduct their business with members through the Center.

Since the Grameen Bank Project was the only channel open to the landless poor for improving their economic status, Yunus included two plans of forced savings in the experiment. He reasoned that the borrowers could not object because they wanted the loans, and when their savings increased they would recognize the value of the program. The program has two segments: the Group (saving) Fund and the Emergency (insurance) Fund.

At the required weekly meeting each member must deposit one *taka* in the Group Fund. This weekly savings can be borrowed against, but can only be withdrawn when a member leaves the group. In addition, when a member receives a loan, five percent of the loan is also put into the Group Fund; all members have an equal right to this portion of the fund, but the money can be withdrawn only after unanimous approval of the group and the GBP field manager.

Bank workers explain the idea behind this enforced saving by using a homely example: if a housewife sets aside one handful of rice each day her family will not notice, but at the end of one year she will have saved a significant amount of grain. Group members have been amazed at the growth of their savings— some Tk.30 million during the first eight years. As Yunus points out, the poor, if given the incentive and the means, *can* save.

Another required saving device is the insurance, or Emergency Fund. Each member pays into the Emergency Fund an amount equal to half the interest charged on his loan. The fund can be tapped in times of personal emergency or disaster, e.g. illness, death of an animal, flood. Group members quickly realize how fortunate they are to have their own money to meet such calamities, rather than being driven into the clutches of a moneylender whose rates can be as high as 10 percent per day.

The group sets its own interest rate for these funds; the only qualification is that the rate must apply equally to all members.

Yunus believes the creation of these two funds explains in part the phenomenal loan repayment rate of 99 percent; for the first time in their lives the poor have financial security, as well as seed money for business enterprises.

In the first two years of the Grameen Bank Project Yunus proved to his own satisfaction that the poor were "bankable," but dealing through the Janata Bank was frustrating because of the paperwork required and the waiting period necessary to obtain the small loans.

An opportunity for gaining the control of the loan operations was provided in 1979 by the Krishi (Agriculture) Bank in Dhaka, a national government institution. In conversation with the Managing Director, A.M. Anisuzzaman, concerning Krishi's ineffectiveness in financing rural development, Yunus offered himself as an experiment. He suggested he be allowed to set up a branch of the bank in Jobra, with Tk.1 million for loans for one year—with no interference from the head office. If he was successful, Krishi could use any of his ideas in the future; if he failed, the bank could write off the experiment as a bad debt.

Despite Anisuzzaman's immediate enthusiasm and agreement, it took almost a year to work out the details. Finally Yunus became the director of a "bank project," rather than a branch bank, in Jobra. He immediately recruited some of his students as bank workers (to replace the commercial bank employees assigned to the Janata project) and at the end of one year he had greatly increased the number of loans given, while maintaining the near-perfect repayment record.

The Central Bank, the government's principal financial institution, took the view that Yunus had accomplished a one-time, one-place, one-person miracle which could not be transferred. The bank challenged him to set up another project in a totally unfamiliar area, and the two parties settled on the Tangail District. The Central Bank agreed to fund the program and Yunus took a leave of absense from the university to become manager of the new bank project.

Field operations in Tangail began in November 1979. The lending program itself was successful but operational costs were high. The project had to hire new workers and rent space either in, or adjacent to, a nationalized commercial bank. Critics pointed to the costs and the low profits which resulted from the small loans. The project itself, however, expanded.

The GBP now attracted international notice. The International Fund for Agricultural Development (IFAD) lent it US$3,400,000 in 1981 for expansion purposes. In 1982 the Ford Foundation gave the GBP a grant of US$125,000 for research and training, and provided a guarantee fund of US$770,000 to be held in the United States in case of loan defaults; this has not been needed.

In early 1983 Yunus felt the GBP had long outgrown its experimental phase. It was a proven success, with 60 branches serving 790 villages in four *thanas*. Therefore the GBP was legally incorporated as the Grameen Bank, with Yunus as Managing Director. Forty percent of its shares were sold to present or former borrowers—one per person at Tk.100 each. Yunus hoped the bank would be completely borrower-owned, but the government insisted on holding 60 percent equity; although having the power, it has not interferred in the bank's operations.

The basis of the bank's funding was a concessional loan from the Central Bank at the same rate of interest given to all commercial banks, and the IFAD loans, of which there have been several, are made through, and matched by, the Central Bank. The Grameen Bank lends at the commercial bank rate (a spread of about 10 percent). It hires employees at competitive salaries and offers career opportunities for both men and women.

By 1989 the bank had over 500 branches operating in 10,000 of the nation's 68,000 villages, with a staff of 1,200 and well over 500,000 borrowers, 85 percent of whom were women. Yunus hopes by 1992 to double the number of branches and loan recipients. The bank disburses close to US$5,000,000 each month in loans limited to Tk.5,000 (US$167), but averaging US$67; the repayment rate is still above 98 percent.

The bank's instructions to its employees are similar to those Yunus gave his bank project helpers in Jobra. Employees must live in the villages in which they work and, apart from a few set hours spent in the office, they must be seen and be available in the village. They are forbidden to take part in forming a group; if anything, their responsibility is to act as the devil's advocate, questioning the composition of the prospective group and challenging its ideas for new enterprises. A business which cannot operator on the local or district market level must be rejected.

The active participation of women in the bank has been a catalyst for change. Women who improve their socioeconomic status are also usually concerned with the future of their children and thus have a heightened awareness of the advantages of health care and education. UNICEF now channels its child health programs through the Centers, and family planning options are available. Customs have been challenged; some groups have agreed to break with the deeply ingrained and costly tradition of dowry.

Yunus is most happy about changes in the types of enterprises being considered by borrowers. Confident in their ability to succeed in small individual businesses, and protected from unforeseen setbacks by their savings and emergency funds, groups are now borrowing for collective—and more profitable—enterprises such as oil or rice mills and machine-operated looms.

In 1984 Muhammad Yunus received the Magsaysay Award for Community Leadership for "enabling the neediest rural men and women to make themselves productive with sound group-managed credit." Since then his voice for credit-assisted self-employment (mircroenterprises) has been heard worldwide—in developed as well as developing nations.

In Chicago Yunus addressed a black social welfare group which in 1988 initiated the Circle Loan Fund and the Women's Self-Employment Project in that city. In Germany he motivated a national youth assocation to develop a credit plan to deal with widespread unemployment. His voice was heard at the subcommittee hearings in 1987 prior to the passage by the U.S. Congress of AID legislation allocating $50 million for credit and other assistance for microenterprises. Developing nations as diverse as Malaysia, Uganda, Pakistan, Mali, Indonesia and Peru have acted upon his concept of extending credit to the very poor.

Yunus received his nation's highest honor, the Independence Day Award, for his contributions to the nation through his unstinting service on national planning boards, such as: Institute of Development Studies, Foundation for Research on Human Resource Development, Panel of Economists advising the National Planning Commission, Education Advisory Committee, Interministerial Committee on Integrated Training program and Committee on Formulating National Strategy for Rural Development.

Nevertheless his heart—and his primary energies—are devoted to the Grameen Bank, which a woman borrower thankfully calls, "God's gift for us."

Indigenous Health Care

Prawase Wasi

"Solving rural poverty is directly related to primary health care. This has been extremely difficult or impossible for most developing countries to understand or achieve, mainly because of fragmented understanding and fragmented approaches to this multidimensional problem."

"Unfortunately, in most developing countries attempts at solving health problems have concentrated on large hospital-based services. This consumes large amounts of resources without proportional return in terms of health and well-being. . . .

"In addition, medicine has been mystified and monopolized; only a handful of health personnel are considered 'health providers,' thus excluding the people and the communities from providing for their own health. This concept and practice results in a very contracted form of health care and hinders health care development. . . ."[1]

Prawase Wasi was born in the town of Kanchanaburi in western Thailand on August 5, 1931, the youngest child of Klai Wasi and Kim Somprasong. Klai made a living cutting bamboo, binding it into rafts and floating it downstream to market. Finding it hard to support his family of four boys and a girl in such

---

1. Prawase Wasi in *My Work, My Teacher*. Ramon Magsaysay Award Foundation: Manila. 1987. pp. 66–67.

fashion, Klai moved to a jungle village and opened a small grocery store, leaving Prawase in Kanchanaburi with relatives to begin his education in the local Buddhist temple school. The short but vital role played by the Buddhist monks in his early life was to have an impact on Prawase Wasi's thinking when, as a distinguished doctor, he sought a means to channel medical care to the rural areas of Thailand.

Although poor, Wasi's parents valued education. Klai had never been to school but he could read and write; his own father—after a hard day of farm work—had taken time at night to teach him. Kim had left school after only six months, but was as keen on the children's education as her husband. (Wasi remembers his mother "as a very strong woman, very decisive, very determined . . . very stable.")

All four sons completed their education to become respectively, a lawyer, an army officer, a pharmacist and a doctor. The daughter, however, the eldest, left school after her primary years to work in the grocery store to help pay for her brothers' education.

Young Prawase contracted malaria during his year in Kanchanaburi so his parents brought him to their village. There he attended the government primary school when it opened the following year. The school, consisting of a packed-earth floor covered by a thatched roof and open to the air on all sides, offered four grades, with all the students studying together.

Prawase completed fourth grade in 1942 and returned to Kanchanaburi to live with an older brother and attend secondary school. He worried constantly that his father was working too hard in order to give him an education; his family, in turn, worried that Wasi was not getting enough to eat, and sent him small sums of money "for treats" each month, which he refused to spend. Years later, when he was studying for his Ph.D. in the United States, his parents were still exhorting him to spend more money on food lest he be too weak to study.

World War II again interrupted Prawase Wasi's schooling for a year, but he graduated in 1947 at the top of his class. From his earliest days family and friends had recognized his scholastic bent and urged him to study to become a doctor, the greatest height, in their eyes, to which he could aspire. Wasi accordingly applied for admission to Triam Udom, one of Bangkok's most prestigious preparatory schools, and was accepted. A village boy, fresh from a disjointed provincial education, he nevertheless stayed in the upper one percent of his class. In 1950 he was accepted in pre-med at Chulalongkorn University, and two years later, in the Faculty of Medicine, Siriraj Hospital, University of Medical Sciences, the oldest and most esteemed medical school in Thailand. The University of Medical Sciences is now known as Mahidol University and includes 14 faculties and institutes in addition to its two medical colleges.

During his years at Siriraj Wasi literally lived at school: he and other students slept in the classrooms, shifting benches together to form beds. Only during his fourth year did Siriraj provide proper dormitories. Despite such conditions, and having to work to pay his tuition, Wasi graduated first in his class.

It was Doctor Prawase Wasi who in 1957 traveled to the United States on a Thai government scholarship to begin graduate study in hematology at the University of Colorado Medical Center in Denver, Colorado. He received his Ph.D. in 1960, and with the money he saved during his stay in Colorado, spent the next six months at the Galton Laboratory of Human Genetics, University of London, England.

During his stay in Denver, Wasi had hoped to study thalassemia—a genetic anemia resulting in a hemoglobin deficiency—which occurs with high frequency in Negro, Mediterranean and Oriental populations. The hematologist at the University of Colorado was not a specialist in this disorder, so Wasi did his research on iron metabolism, lymphoid leukemia, and leukemia and lymphoma in mice, writing his doctoral dissertation on the latter.

When he returned to Thailand in 1961 Wasi was appointed a professor at Siriraj Medical School. Eight years later, at the age of 38, he married one of his former students, Chantapong Prakobpol, who is herself a prominent virologist at Siriraj.

Wasi not only proved to be an outstanding professor, and was honored as such by his students in 1969, but he has made major contributions in the field of hematology. In 1967 he received the first of many annual grants for research in thalassemia from the U.S. National Institutes of Health, and in 1973 he was invited to

become a member of the Panel of Experts on Abnormal Hemo-
globins and Thalassemia, International Committee for the Stan-
dardization of Diagnostic Materials. He has published over 100
articles in the field, a textbook (1968) and a handbook (1975).
Because of his work and reputation the World Health Organization (WHO) designated the Hematology Division of Siriraj Hospital as an international training center for medical specialists
and scientists.

In his first years at Siriraj Wasi undertook field research on
the prevalence of anemia and thalassemia among Thailand's
rural communities. The teams he led surveyed the occurence of
hemoglobin E, a mild form of anemia that is only lethal when it
interacts with thalassemia. These studies showed that hemoglobin E, while affecting only 13 percent of the population in
Bangkok, affects more than 50 percent of the population in the
country's rural northeastern quadrant.

Another study he undertook was of hemoglobin H disease,
also known to be related to alpha thalassemia, but whose genetic
mechanism was not understood. A child with hemoglobin H
disease could have parents, only one of whom would have
abnormal appearing red cells. Wasi concluded that the apparently normal parent must be carrying another type of alpha
thalassemia gene, so mild it could not be detected. He and his
team published their hypothesis in 1964 in the British scientific
journal *Nature*. The hypothesis has since been confirmed, and
the two different genes are known as Wasi's alpha thalassemia-
1, and Wasi's alpha thalassemia-2. Wasi's reputation as one of
the world's leading hematologists was thus firmly established.

Wasi's interest in thalassemia, however, goes beyond a scientific study of the disease; it is intimately related to his concern
for the sufferers in rural Thailand.

There are more than 60 forms of thalassemia in Thailand,
whose effects range from few or no symptoms to lethal. In one
form of alpha thalassemia, in which a fetus inherits an alpha
thalassemia gene from each parent, all victims die, either *in
utero* or a few minutes after birth. In other types, babies become
anemic after three months, their livers and spleens enlarge, the
bone changes, growth is retarded and they die between the ages

of five and ten. Conversely, people with mild cases can survive to old age.

Sometimes two cases caused by the same combination of genes can exhibit very different degrees of severity. Wasi and other scientists at Siriraj are still trying to discover what other factors determine the severity in an individual case. They hope to be able to manipulate severe cases into mild ones. Wasi has contacted large pharmaceutical firms to persuade them to support basic investigation into the nature of enzymes, with the hope of finding drugs which will increase the proteolytic activity in the red cells. He is also engaged in a study of genetic engineering by means of which he hopes to reduce the severity of the disease.

Wasi's field studies in thalassemia ironically led to a profound and lasting concern for the *general health* of the rural population. When his teams went into the provinces, villagers flocked to them for treatment of a multitude of diseases. Modern medical care had not reached —and indeed would not as far as he could foresee—these poverty-striken villages, far from the provincial capitals. And the hospitals in the provincial capitals, he found, like the large public hospitals in Bangkok, were so swamped with patients that "medical care," all too frequently, meant no more than a minute's examination by the doctor of the patients who had stood in line for hours to see him.

Thailand's medical services were topsy-turvy. Ideally, Wasi was convinced, national health services should be a broad-based triangle, divided into four unequal parts. The wide base of the triangle should be *primary health care,* where "people and communities are able to help themselves in taking care of their own health, in curing their own sicknesses and those of other people around." The next level should be *primary medical care,* consisiting of small health centers or hospitals with one or two doctors—if necessary only a nurse and assistants—whose services would be available to people in their own or nearby villages. The narrower part of the triangle should consist of *secondary medical care,* based on large general provincial hospitals, and the tip should be *tertiary medical care* delivered by specialists.

In Thailand, however, as in so many developing countries, the triangle was reversed. There were many specialists, fewer general hospitals, and few small health centers; *primary health care* was the most neglected segment of all. At the same time modern education was teaching people *not to take care of themselves,* but to see a doctor when they were ill. Yet as late as 1981 there were only 8,000 doctors to serve roughly 48 million Thai.

The situation was compounded by the fact that doctors did not want to serve in rural districts, where they were unable to supplement their salaries with private practice as they could in urban centers. Consequently half the doctors remained in Bangkok. This meant that Bangkok had a doctor/patient ratio of roughtly 1:1,100, whereas in the provinces the ratio was 1:10,900. Wasi blamed this gap—which was far more severe when he began his career—on the system of education which failed to inculcate in medical students an understanding of Thailand's public health problem.

To help correct the situation he and two doctors from the other two leading medical schools, Chulalongkorn and Ramathibodi, addressed a memorandum to the prime minister in 1971, suggesting a reformation of the public medical school system. They stated that teaching-doctors were not spending enough time with their students (or with their patients) because the bureaucratic system gave them absolute job security. They proposed, therefore, a system be adopted whereby doctor-teachers would be appointed for 1–3 years and then evaluated to determine whether or not they should be kept on the faculty.

The cabinet approved the memorandum and returned it through channels to the medical schools, with a note requesting more details. There the letter created an uproar and the three doctors found themselves subject to severe harassment. The matter eventually reached the king, who recommended that any change be agreed upon by the teachers involved—in effect nullifying the proposal. Wasi realized that the rigidity of the bureaucracy was the single greatest obstacle to the promotion of a viable public health system.

Not discouraged, he took a new approach to the problem of bringing the medical system in line with reality. He had been elected to a second term as a member of the Medical Council of Thailand and was chairman of the subcommittee to recommend a national health plan. Working closely with the Minister and

Deputy Minister of Public Health on proposals to reform the public health system, he urged that the system rely more on traditional indigenous medicine and treatment than on imported drugs and equipment.

He and colleagues also suggested the establishment of a new medical school which would offer an alternative curriculum, emphasizing service to humanity, and teaching science and technology as tools rather than goals. Prior to being accepted for medical training, prospective students would be required to work in and *be accepted by* the rural community; their medical training would be in district and provincial, rather than university, hospitals. Once again Wasi found his proposals blocked by the establishment, although the program in no way threatened existing schools. (An approach similar to that of Wasi and his friends was conceived independently by Dr. Moshe Prywes of Israel, and has been successfully implemented there.)

Wasi's efforts to redistribute the nation's doctors finally began to bear fruit by the late 1970s, with young interns and doctors volunteering for provincial service in numbers greater than there were government hospital positions available. Some did so to escape military service, but the majority were highly motivated. Many ascribe this change to Wasi's teaching and his continuing pressure on the government. Wasi himself modestly ascribes it to the success of the student movement in 1973 that effectively brought students into the political mainstream.

Wasi next directed his energies to convincing the government to construct the 370 new hospitals necessary to provide one in each of the nation's 670 districts. His attempts to right the upside down health care triangle also led him to speak out against proposals to build large hospitals. One such project proposed building four 1,000-bed hospitals, one in each section of the country; another called for a very large hospital in Don Muang on the outskirts of Bangkok. In both cases, the hospitals were to be called "King's hospitals," a ploy intended to win them support. This, however, did not prevent Wasi from publicly disagreeing with the projects—which would have further concentrated doctors in major urban centers instead of dispersing them to the outlying rural districts where they were so sorely needed.

Correcting the maldistribution of doctors is one way of adjusting the health care triangle; expanding *primary health care* is another. In 1981 Wasi estimated that one percent of Thailand's population was sick enough each day to need medical attention. He believed that fully 90 percent of these illnesses were preventable, that they were caused by poverty, poor sanitation or poor health education. But good primary health care, Wasi insists, must involve all sectors of the community. Ideally each community of about 1,000 families should have its own health care center staffed by a nurse, a health worker, and a midwife. Since this goal has not yet been achieved, the government has trained a corps of "village health volunteers." These volunteers are farmers or housewives who are taught to treat common illnesses; refer patients requiring further treatment to a health center or district hospital; keep health records; and inform the health officer of endemic diseases.

Even though this is a move in the right direction, Wasi has long felt part-time efforts of volunteers—who must also eke out a living—are not sufficient. Therefore in recent years he has developed different techniques to promote health care in the villages.

With others he has published a number of health manuals. The first, *Handbook for Health of the People* (Khuumeu Kandulaeraksaa Sukhapaap Samrap Prachachon), was edited by him, and written by him and 10 other prominent physicians, pharmacists and public health officials. To give it cachet it was published on the occasion of the king's 48th birthday (1975). It's premise is that the people should be given the information necessary to treat themselves. The following year he wrote and published *Public Health for the Masses* (Kansatharanasuk peua Muanchon). In 1978 a compilation of health columns he had written for a popular magazine was issued under the title *Household Doctor* (Moh Prachamabaan). Continuing in this vein he published *Thai Medical Record* (Bantheuk Wechakaam Thai, 1981), a small volume of case studies which were presented in simple and popular fashion to illustrate how medical science can be self-defeating if it does not concern itself with economics, religion, ethics and the patients' overall mental and physical state. A good doctor, the book implies, must know the whole person if he is to cure him.

Perhaps most importantly, in 1979 Wasi became publisher and editor of the monthly *Folk Doctor Magazine* (Moh Chao Baam), which provides "self-curing knowledge and knowledge on primary health care to the public." Two years later the Folk Doctor Foundation was established, under whose auspices the magazine is now published. A major portion of the US$20,000 Ramon Magsaysay Government Service Award that Wasi received in 1981 for "his research contributions to medical science while prompting his profession to make modern health care available to the poor," was given to the Folk Doctor Foundation. The foundation publishes other learning materials, runs a radio program and participates in expanding the training of monks—a project undertaken by Wasi in recent years.

Folk Doctor Magazine is addressed to the common man, as well as to health communicators: teachers, monks, district doctors and health personnel, and village health volunteers. Its aim is to demystify medicine and transfer medical technology to the people. Teaching basic medical and health sciences, it explains in simple terms how to make diagnoses and how to treat simple illnesses. It lists medicines—directions for taking them, possible side effects and reasonable prices—to cure common ailments such as headache, stomachache, diarrhea and malaria. Herbs used in traditional medical treatment are discussed along with modern synthetic medicines.

The magazine has a monthly circulation of over 50,000 and is supported by donations, and by subscribers such as WHO which gave an initial one-year subscription to 12,000 village health volunteers. The magazine depends less on advertisements than most periodicals since it is selective in its advertisers and lists the fair market price of drugs, a practice that does not endear it to pharmaceutic concerns. Nevertheless it broke even in only two years.

At the time Wasi began the magazine Thailand was importing 26,000 brands of drugs and vaccines worth US$500 million. Many were of unknown quality, with possible deleterious side effects, and available without prescription or supervision by a doctor.

In addition, the very popular *Ya-chood* (sets of imported drugs) were sold illegally for common ailments. *Ya-chood* are sold in packets, without identification or directions for use, and many combinations are potentially dangerous. Wasi estimates that annually 4,000 to 5,000 tons of drugs are *unnecessarily* consumed through this practice of combining drugs, on the theory that if one won't cure, another may.

Wasi began his campaign against the importation of the massive number and amount of drugs shortly after WHO issued its 1977 list of 225 drugs it considered essential for the vast majority of health problems of Third World countries. The Thai Ministry of Public Health also published a National Essential Drug List, but the application of both sets of recommendations was met with resistance, even by certain authorities. Therefore, in order to combat abuses, and to reduce the dependence on foreign drugs, Wasi undertook to investigate and promote the use of traditional herbal medicines of proven value and dosage.

Thailand is an overwhelmingly Buddhist country, with over 90 percent of the people professing that faith. The concept of social responsibility on the part of Buddhists is a matter of debate. Sociologists have noted that many Buddhists turn their backs on social problems because of a deepseated belief that a person's present condition is the result of his actions in this or in previous lives: each person must cope with his own *karma* (fate)—it cannot be changed by anyone else. A devout Buddhist himself, Wasi maintains on the contrary: "According to the Lord Buddha's teaching, each of us has the clear purpose of helping his fellows, both spiritually and physically. Only in this way can we hope to raise our own spiritual level."

Regardless of the interpretation of responsibility by the layman, the obligation of community service has traditionally been accepted by the Buddhist *sangha* (monkhood). Temples were centers for education (e.g. Wasi's first primary school), for the treatment of the sick, and for cultural activities. However with the adoption of modern Western attitudes many of these activities were taken over by the government. The *sangha* consequently found itself in a critical position. It could withdraw into itself, as many monasteries have, and concentrate on building finer temples and more comfortable living quarters; or it could recapture its traditional role of service.

Taking the lead in the latter, two Buddhist universities, Mahamakutra and Mahachulalongkorn, began adjusting their curricula in the mid-1960s to prepare monks for educational and community service. In the late 60s and early 70s, Sangha Education and Development Centers were established in every province of the northeast, and in Chiang Mai in the north, to train rural monk-leaders in technical subjects related to community development. Progress was slow until 1975 when Wasi was invited to give the annual lecture of the Komol Keemthong Foundation, a foundation on whose board he has long served. His speech, "How the Monks and Lay Buddhists Can Restore the Nation," was received enthusiastically and has been frequently reprinted. That same year the foundation collaborated with the abbot of Wat Thongnopakun to start a class to train monks in primary health care. The course, designed by Wasi, was divided into eight basic sectors: food and nutrition; clean water and sanitation; immunization; mother and child health; control of endemic diseases; treatment of common injuries and illnesses; provision of essential drugs, and health education.

When the course proved successful, Wasi suggested expansion of the program to the Ministry of Public Health. He was met with agreement in principle, but a bureaucratic inability to act. The Komol Keemthong Foundation, and later the Folk Doctor Foundation, decided to continue the training program on their own. In so doing they had the cooperation of influential monks. One of these, the abbot of Wat Samphraya, became so interested in the project that he declared the aim of the *sangha* should be to have all of the some 200,000 monks in the country attend the course.

When Wasi observed, "Your goal is very high; what is your budget?", and the abbot replied, "Nothing," Wasi was interested. If the abbot could run the course on no budget it could run forever! The secret was simple, the abbot pointed out: monks travel without charge, stay in temples, and are fed by the people. With such basic needs taken care of, surely, he said, the foundation could pick up the cost of the program. Wasi agreed, and Wat Samphraya became the site for a series of courses, offered monthly to 50 monks at a time.

Wasi finds teaching monks stimulating. Medical students have few or no questions at the end of a lecture because they have never been exposed to "real problems of real people." Monks, on the other hand, who have no scientific background but are constantly exposed to the realities of life, are full of questions and eager to learn. Furthermore, they can often answer practical questions that the teacher himself can not. For example, a monk asked Wasi how to cure warts. Wasi could not give him an answer because the modern physician's cure—silver nitrate— was not available in rural villages. But another monk spoke up: he knew a plant that consistently produced a cure. This, Wasi notes, is true education, a multilateral rather than a unilateral teaching/learning process.

The work of monks, however, has certain inherent limitations. A monk can advocate inoculations for women but cannot give them, since he is prohibited from bodily contact with the female sex. He can advocate the distribution of nutritional food, but cannot prepare food himself. He can distribute medicines, but is not allowed to receive direct reimbursement for them. Still it is in this area of distribution of essential drugs that Wasi expects monks to be most helpful.

No person or organization can provide, free of charge, enough drugs to supply the continuing needs of 50,000 Thai villages. A continuing channel for the supply of drugs is necessary and monasteries offer that channel. It is the custom in Thailand that people from cities visit rural temples at least once a year with donations of money and new robes; Wasi urges that instead of money and clothes they donate drugs. The temples are now providing a list of those needed.

Another health-care conduit is the dispenser of traditional Thai medicine—men still found in virtually every village. In recent years these practitioners have been invited to share with monks their knowledge of curative herbs and plants, and are in turn given the opportunity by Wasi and his colleagues of having their own training upgraded to include basic Western health care.

In 1979, when Wasi organized a seminar on traditional medicine at Siriraj University, it was discovered that laws regulating the practice of herbal medicine prevented the acceptance and adaptation of new ideas. One law decreed that traditional medicine must be practiced in the traditional way, *with no change in methodology.* A direct result of the seminar's findings was that the university and the Ministry of Public Health examined the laws relating to medicine as a whole, found many were out of date and needed to be amended, and took action to change them.

Wasi's attitude toward medicine centers around two related concepts. The first is self-reliance: of the individual, of the community, of the nation. The second is that rural poverty and primary health care are directly related. To illustrate his theses, Wasi tells of a young abbot who was sent to a wat in the village of Yokkrabutr, Samutsakhon Province, a poor community whose young people fled to Bangkok as soon as they could. Instead of being discouraged, the abbot studied ways to improve the economic life of the village. He decided that the region was suitable for raising coconuts and in his sermons began advocating so doing. Soon the entire community was involved in planting a strain of coconut with a high yield of sugar syrup. The village prospered, temple donations increased, and the abbot was able to start a second project, providing the village with unpolluted water. In such a way, even without a doctor, the health of the community improved. The villagers drank pure water and had money to buy good and sufficient food. Ergo, their health improved since food and clean water made them more resistant to the myriad diseases that plague the rural poor.

The abbot's assumption of the correlation between poverty and disease has been proven by studies. In one study done by Wasi, four groups of people from different economic levels were examined for anemia: medical students, nursing students, and two groups of farmers. The medical students, who are usually from financially comfortable families, showed no signs of anemia, while nursing students, generally from poorer homes, tested 11 percent. Forty percent of the farmers living 50 kilometers from Bangkok proved to be anemic, and 90 percent of those in the northeast, the poorest section the country, were

suffering from this disorder. Poverty—and ignorance—Wasi re-
iterates time and again, are major health problems.

The solutions to these problems, however, are far from simple. Wasi believes that Thailand needs socially-conscious political movements, a broad program of health education and, above
all, a more flexible, people-oriented bureaucratic system. As it
is presently structured, the bureaucratic system still inhibits
community development, which he considers the key to the
country's overall development. "If Thailand's problems can not
be solved in the village," Wasi insists, "they can not be solved
at all." Ideally, he maintains, community development should
be like health care, a triangle, with the local community the
broad base, and the central bureaucracy the tip.

Although not all of Wasi's ideas have been implemented, he
is not "a voice crying in the wilderness." As Head of the
Department of Medicine at the Faculty of Medicine Siriraj
Hospital, and Director of the National Coordinating Center for
Medical and Health Affairs, Wasi is playing a leading role in
changing Thailand's approach to rural health. As Chairman of
WHO's Southeast Asia Advisory Committee for Health Research his influence is being felt throughout Southeast Asia, and
through the International Advisory Committee he has recommended that WHO tackle the worldwide problem of rural poverty in the holistic, participatory manner he advocates in Thailand.

In 1981 Wasi received the Magsaysay Award for Government
Service for his "research contributions to medical science while
prompting his profession to make modern health care available
to the poor." He was named Thai Scientist of the Year two years
later and in 1985 was chosen Thailand's Outstanding Person in
Medicine. Wasi has published four books during the past decade:
*Records of Thai Medical Practice; Buddhism and Society; How
to Get Rid of Boredom and Create Happiness;* and *Happiness
for All,* thus synthesizing his holistic approach to medicine and
to life itself.

References

ABED, FAZLE HASAN

Abed, Fazle Hasan. "Approaches to Mobilizing Villagers' Latent Capabilities." Presentation to Group Discussion. Ramon Magsaysay Award Foundation, Manila. September 2, 1980. (Typewritten Transcript).

Bangladesh Rural Advancement Committee. Brochure. Dhaka: BRAC Printers. November 1983; June 1985; September 1986.

Brehmer, Margaret, *et al.* "Anandapur Village: BRAC Comes to Town," *Reports.* Dacca: Bangladesh Rural Advancement Committee (BRAC). No. 13. November 1976.

"BRAC, Summary of Current Activities." *Ibid.*

Clark, Leon. "A Consultant's Journal: Bangladesh," *Ibid.*

Faaland, Just and J. R. Parkinson. *Bangladesh: the Test Case of Development.* Bangladesh: C. Hurst and Co. and University Press Ltd. 1976.

"Jamalpur Women's Programme." Dacca: BRAC. N.d. (Mimeographed).

"Manikganj Project Report, Phase I (April 1976–March 1979)." Dacca: BRAC. N.D. (Mimeographed).

"Mirfur Bastuhara Resettlement Programme." Dacca: BRAC. August 1978. (Mimeographed).

"Peasant Perceptions: Famine." Dacca: BRAC. July 1979. (Mimeographed).

"Sulla Project: Report on Phase II, November 1, 1972–December 31, 1975." Dacca: BRAC. N.d. (Mimeographed).

179

"Sulla Project: Report on Phase III." Dacca: BRAC. 1975. (Mimeographed).

Transcripts of extensive interviews with Fazle Hasan Abed and others acquainted with him and with his work, and reports on visits to BRAC, are available at the Ramon Magsaysay Center, Manila, Philippines.

BHATT, CHANDI PRASAD

Albert, David. "Hugging Trees: The Growth of India's Movement," *WIN Magazine*. Brooklyn, N.Y. November 22, 1979.

Bahuguna, Sunderlal. "Chipko," *Voluntary Action*. New Delhi. June 1978.

———. "Chipko Movement." Address to Golden Jubilee Celebration of the Himalaya Club of India. International Center, New Delhi. February 19, 1978.

———. "Himalayan Trauma: Forests, Faults, Floods—Chipko Seeks a New Policy." Ganga-Brahmaputra Workshop Working Paper No. 29. N.d.

Bhatt, Chandi Prasad. "The Chipko Experience." International Conference on Environmental Education. N.d.

———. *Eco-System of the Central Himalayas and Chipko Movement*. Gopeshwar, India: Dasholi Gram Swarajya Sangh. August 1980.

———. "Protecting the Wise Use of Forests." Presentation to Group Discussion. Ramon Magsaysay Award Foundation, Manila. September 2, 1982.

———. "Trees—a Source of Energy for Village Dwellers." Paper delivered at the Non-governmental Organizations Forum on New and Renewable Sources of Energy, Nairobi, Kenya. August 9–16, 1981.

Das, J. C. and R. S. Negi. "The Chipko Movement," *Anthropological Survey of India*. Calcutta. September 1976.

Dasholi Gram Swarajya Sangh. "Afforestation Programs in Chamoli Hill District, Uttar Pradesh." N.d. (Typewritten).

Joshi, Gopa. "Afforestation of Deforested Himalayas," *HOW/KAISE*. New Delhi. April 1981.

————. "Women and the Chipko Movement." N.d. (Typewritten).

Kumar, Kamlesh and Mata Deen. "Environmental Degradation in Himalayan Region." Paper presented at I.G.U. International Symposium on Energy Resources, Environment and Habitat Transformation in Developing Countries. Meerut University, Meerut, India. March 1982.

Kunwar, Sishupal Singh, ed. *Hugging the Himalayas: The Chipko Experience.* Gopeshwar, Uttar Pradesh, India: Dasholi Gram Swarajya Mandal. March 1982.

Mishra, Anupam. "Tree Plantation Camps in Himalayas," *Changing Environment Newsletter.* New Delhi: Gandhi Peace Foundation. February 1981.

Shepard, Mark. "Chipko: North India's Tree Huggers," *The CoEvolution Quarterly.* Sausalito, California. Fall 1981.

Tripathi, N. P. "Chipko Movement—State Government's View." Paper for presentation to H. M. Patel, Union Minister for Home during his visit to Dudhwa National Park, Nainital, Uttar Pradesh, March 10–11, 1979.

Trivedi, P. P. "Report of Planning Commission Multi Level Planning Unit Tour of the Uttar Pradesh Hill Area, January 28–February 2, 1982." (Typewritten).

Verghese, B. G. "Repairing a Ravaged Himalay," *Voluntary Action.* New Delhi. July/August 1979.

Transcripts of extensive interviews with Chandi Prasad Bhatt and persons acquainted with him, his life and his work, and reports on a visit to Gopeshwar and vicinity available at the Ramon Magsaysay Center, Manila, Philippines.

CHOWDHURY, ZAFRULLAH

Chowdhury, Zafrullah. "Affordable and Effective Rural Community Health Service." Presentation made to Group Discussion. Ramon Magsaysay Award Foundation, Manila. September 3, 1985. (Typewritten transcript.)

————. "Basic Service Delivery in 'Underdeveloping Countries': A View from Gonoshasthaya Kendra." Working paper for United Nations Children's Fund Special Meeting on the Situation of Children in Asia with Emphasis on Basic Services. May 4, 1977.

————. "Research: A Method of Colonialization," *Bangladesh Times*. January 13, 14, 1977.

"Drug Policy Saves *Taka 30 Crore*," *Bangladesh Observer*. March 24, 1985.

Gonoshasthaya Pharmaceuticals. Brochure. Savar, Bangladesh: Gonoshasthaya Pharmaceuticals. N.d.

Rolt, Fracis. *Pills, Policies and Profits*. London: War on Want. 1985.

Thomas, Winburn T., ed. *An Evaluative Study of People's Health Center's Health Plan (Gonoshasthaya Kendra)*. Dhaka, Bangladesh: International Voluntary Services, Inc. June 1, 1974.

Transcripts of extensive interviews with Zafrullah Chowdhury and persons acquainted with him and his work available at the Ramon Magsaysay Center, Manila, Philippines.

DESAI, MANIBHAI BHIMBHAI

Beresford, Tristram. "The Case of Uruli-Kanchan: A Study in Development," *Journal of Agricultural Economics*. Kent, England: Agricultural Economics Society. Vol. 24, no. 1, 1973.

Chopra, Pran. "Aforestation: A Success Story," *Indian Express*. Bangalore, India. September 19, 1980.

————. "Regenerating the Rural Economy," *Indian Express*. Bombay. October 6, 1980.

Desai, Manibhai Bhimbhai. "Background Story of BAIF." Lecture delivered at Government of India Workshop on Integrated Rural Development through Cross-breeding of Cattle under DPAP Program. Pune, India. August 1, 1977.

————. "Exclusively for You from the Director's Cell," *BAIF Journal*. Pune, India. Vol. 2, no. 1, October 2, 1981.

————. "Growing Scarcity of Fodder and Fuel," *Commerce*. Bombay. Vol. 143, no. 3670, October 17, 1981.

————. "Helping the Man on the Land." Presentation to Group Discussion. Ramon Magsaysay Award Foundation, Manila. September 1, 1982.

Kubabul [subabul], the Miracle Plant. Brochure. Pune: BAIF. (N.d.).

Marulkar, R. P. "Gandhiji's Unique Rural Scheme," *Indian Express*. Bombay. August 25, 1980.

Relawani, L. L. "Subabul, the Superb Fuelwood Tree," *Science Today*. Bombay. Vol. 15, no. 10, October 1981.

Relawani, L. L. and D. V. Rangnekar. "The Second Green Revolution," *Ibid*.

Rural Liabilities Become Productive Assets the BAIF Way. Pamphlet. Uruli-Kanchan, Pune: BAIF. 1981.

Transcripts of extensive interviews with Manibhai Bhimbhai Desai and persons acquainted with him and his work, and report on visit to Uruli-Kanchan available at the Ramon Magsaysay Center, Manila, Philippines.

KAWAKITA, JIRO

Dutto, Carl A. "The Arduous Trail To Rural Development," *Foreign Service Journal*. Washington, D.C.: American Foreign Service Association. May 1988.

Kawakita, Jiro. *Cultural Ecology of Nepal Himalaya*. Tokyo: ATCHA (Association for Technical Cooperation to the Himalayan Areas). February 1984.

————. *The Original KJ Method*. Tokyo: KJ Method Headquarters, Kawakita Research Institute. 1982.

————. *A proposal for the Revitalization of Rural Areas, Based on Ecology and Participation*. Tokyo: ATCHA. February 1984.

————. "Technical Assistance in the Himalayas," *The Wheel Extended*. Tokyo: Toyota Motor Sales Co., Ltd. Special Issue: Summer 1975.

————. "Technology with Environmental Conservation: The Sikha Valley Experience." Presentation to Group Discussion, Ramon Magsaysay Award Foundation, Manila. September 1, 1984. (Typewritten transcript).

Mori, M., Jiro Kawakita and K. Ogawa. *Natural Force Propulsion Boats*. Tokyo: ATCHA. May 1984.

Transcripts of extensive interviews with Jiro Kawakita and persons acquainted with him and his work available at the Ramon Magsaysay Center, Manila, Philippines.

McGLINCHEY, PATRICK J.

Ayers, James. "How You Get 'Em Down to the Farm," *Pacific Stars and Stripes*. Tokyo. January 22, 1973.

"Cheju Island," *Report to the Government of the Republic of Korea on Possibilities for Development of Range, Pasture and Fodder Resources*. November 1970.

"Irish Priest Explains Success in Ranch," *Korea Times*. Seoul. June 6, 1972.

"Isidore Farm Welcomes Australia Cattle," *Korea Herald*. Seoul. January 26, 1973.

Kelly, Father Jerry. "Dreams Come True," *Guideposts*. Korean Edition. Vol. 10, no. 1.

Lincoln, Tom. "Father McGlinchey's 'Flock' on Cheju," *Pacific Stars and Stripes*. Tokyo. October 1, 1972.

McGlinchey, Patrick J. Transcript of Presentation to Group Discussion. Ramon Magsaysay Award Foundation, Manila. September 3, 1975.

Murphy, Sunny. "Cheju Do—Korea's Island Province," *AWC Journal*. Seoul. January–February 1973.

Yun, Ik-Han. "Missionary Worker Fights Farm Poverty," *Korea Herald*. Seoul. June 11, 1972.

Transcripts of interviews with Father Patrick J. McGlinchey and those acquainted with his work, and report on visit to Isidore Development Association projects, Cheju Island, available at the Ramon Magsaysay Center, Manila, Philippines.

RAMON MAGSAYSAY AWARD FOUNDATION

Abueva, Jose Veloso. *Ramon Magsaysay: A Political Biography*. Manila: Solidaridad Publishing House. 1971.

Manahan, Manuel P. "Unforgettable Ramon Magsaysay," *Reader's Digest*. Asian Edition. November 1987.

Ramon Magsaysay Award Foundation. *The Ramon Magsaysay Awards*. Manila. Eight volumes: 1958–1984.

Ramon Magsaysay Award Foundation papers and files. Ramon Magsaysay Center, Manila, Philippines.

SOEDJARWO, ANTON

Dian Desa: Appropriate Technology Group. Yogyakarta: Dian Desa Institute. N.d.

Kaufman, Marcus. *From Lorena to a Mountain of Fire.* Yogyakarta: Yayasan Dian Desa. 1983.

Report: Sharing of Traditional Technology. Yogyakarta: Dian Desa Institute. 1980.

Roy, A. D. "Report on Mission to the Republic of Indonesia, July 3–10, 1979," *United Nations Development Programme Global Project GLO/78/006.* September 1979.

Sharing of Traditional Technology: Report of the Post Pilot Phase Study. Yogyakarta: Dian Desa Institute. December 1979.

Soedjarwo, Anton. "People's Participation in Community Development." Presentation to Group Discussion. Ramon Magsaysay Award Foundation, Manila. September 1, 1983. (Typewritten transcript).

Teknologi Tepat: Pengawatan Telur (Appropriate Technology: Preserving Eggs). In Indonesian. Yogyakarta: Yayasan Dian Desa. N.d.

United Nations University: Project Meeting, Sharing of Traditional Technology. Yogyakarta: Dian Desa Institute. April 16–22, 1979.

Wachtel, Paul Spencer. "Indonesia's 'Light of the Village,' " *Reader's Digest.* April 1981.

William, Glenn. *Yayasan Dian Desa: Appropriate Technology Programme, 4th Report, Period January–July 1977.* Report to OXFAM. (Typewritten).

Transcripts of extensive interviews with Anton Soedjarwo and persons acquainted with him and his work and reports on visits to Dian Desa headquarters and projects available at the Ramon Magsaysay Center, Manila, Philippines.

WASI, PRAWASE

Chu, Valentin. *Thailand Today: A Visit to Modern Siam.* New York: T. Y. Crowell. 1968.

Gosling, David. "Thailand's Bare-headed Doctors," *Modern Asian Studies.* Cambridge, England: Cambridge University Press. Vol. 19, no. 4, 1985.

Insor, D. *Thailand: A Political, Social and Economic Analysis.* New York: Praeger. 1963.

"I'm My Own Doctor," *Bangkok World.* June 8, 1978.

International Bank for Reconstruction and Development. *Public Development Program for Thailand.* Baltimore: Johns Hopkins Press. 1959.

Klausner, William. "The Thai Sangha and National Development," *Visakha Puja B.E. 2521.* Bangkok: Buddhist Association of Thailand. May 1978.

Sulayakanond, Wirasak. "Health Means Wealth," *Bangkok World.* September 23, 1979.

Wasi, Prawase. "Bareheaded Doctors," *World Health.* July 1986.

―――. "Public Health for the Masses," *Sociological Society Journal of Thailand.* Bangkok. 1976.

―――. "The Sangha and Medical Care: An Appreciation," *Visakha Puja, B.E. 2522.* Bangkok: Buddhist Association of Thailand. May 1979.

Transcripts of extensive interviews with Prawase Wasi and persons acquainted with him and his work available at the Ramon Magsaysay Center, Manila, Philippines.

WATSON, HAROLD RAY

Watson, Harold Ray. "SALT and FAITH for the Poor Farmers." Presentation to Group Discussion. Ramon Magsaysay Award Foundation, Manila. September 4, 1985. (Typewritten transcript.)

Watson, Harold R., and Warlito A. Laquihon. *How to Farm Better.* Davao, Philippines: Mindanao Baptist Rural Life Center. 1984.

―――. *How to Farm Your Hilly Land Without Losing Your Soil.* Davao, Philippines: Mindanao Baptist Rural Life Center. 1984.

―――. *How to Make FAITH (Food Always in the Home) Garden.* Davao, Philippines: Mindanao Baptist Rural Life Center. 1983.

―――. *Sloping Agricultural Land Technology SALT) as Developed by the Mindanao Baptist Rural Life Center.* Paper presented at the Workshop on the Site Protection and Amelioration Roles of Agroforestry, Institute of Forest

Conservation, University of Philippines at Los Banos, September 4–11, 1985. (Mimeographed.)

Transcripts of extensive interviews with Reverend Harold Ray Watson and persons acquainted with his work, and reports on visits to the Mindanao Baptist Rural Life Center, are available at the Ramon Magsaysay Center, Manila, Philippines.

YUNUS, MUHAMMAD

Buell, Becky. "Credit Where Credit is Due: The Grameen Banks' Recipe for Development," *Turning the Tables on Development: Grassroots Solution to Hunger and Poverty*. San Francisco: Food First Books. 1989.

Alamgir, Mohiuddin. "Report on Grameen Bank Project" (part of a report prepared by the International Fund for Agricultural Development mission). Dhaka: Grameen Bank. April 1982.

Claiborne, William. "Bangladesh Landless Prove Credit-Worthy," *Washington Post*. March 19, 1984.

Darshini, Priya. "A Bank That Has the Poor As Its Clients," *Asian Monitor*. New York. March 9, 1984.

Government of Bangladesh Agricultural Credit Review. Dhaka. August 1983.

Harley, Richard. "Special Report: The Entrepreneurial Poor," *Food Ford Foundation Letter*. New York. Vol. 14, no. 3, June 1, 1983.

Fuglesang, Andreas and Dale Chandler. *Participation as Process: What We Can Learn from Grameen Bank, Bangladesh*. Dhaka: Grameen Bank. 1988.

Hossian, Mahabub. "Credit for Alleviation of Rural Poverty: The Grameen Bank in Bangladesh," *International Food Policy Research Institute*. Research Report 65. Washington, D.C. February 1988.

———. "Issues Concerning Employment Expansion in Noncrop Activities in Bangladesh." Bangkok: ARTEP, International Labor Organization. 1982. (Mimeographed).

Miyan, A. H. and V. U. Qintana. *A Study of Bangladesh Krishi Bank-Grameen Bank Project*. Bangladesh Krishi Bank Central Training Institute. 1981.

Rahman, Atiur and S. M. Hossain. "Demand Constraints and the Future Viability of Grameen Bank Credit Programme—An Econometric Study of the Expenditure Pattern of Rural Households," *The Bangladesh Development Studies*. Vol. 16, no. 2, June 1988.

Roberts, Brad. "Participation: A Pragmatic Agenda for the 1990s," *Significant Issues Series*. Washington, D.C.: Center for Strategic and International Studies. Vol. 9, no. 10.

Quasim, M. A. *et al. Impact of Grameen Bank Project Operation on Landless Women*. Bangladesh Institute of Bank Management. December 1981.

Yunus, Muhammad. "Banking for the Landless." Presentation to Group Discussion. Ramon Magsaysay Award Foundation, Manila. September 3, 1984.

———. *Credit for Self-Employment: A Fundamental Human Right*. Dhaka: Grameen Bank. May 1987.

———. "Foreword," *Annual Report: Grameen Bank Project*. 1980–1988. Dhaka.

———. "Measures Needed to Make the Poverty Focused Programs More Effective in Reaching the Poor." Paper presented at Project Implementation Workshop, International Fund for Agricultural Development, Delhi. April 1984.

Transcripts of extensive interviews with Muhammad Yunus and persons acquainted with him and his work, and copies of numerous Bangladeshi and Western newspaper and magazine articles, available at the Ramon Magsaysay Center, Manila, Philippines.

Index